MOS Study Guide for
Microsoft Word
Exam MO-100

Joan Lambert

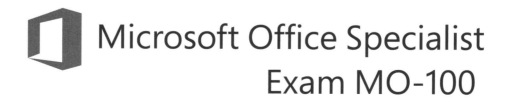

Microsoft Office Specialist
Exam MO-100

MOS Study Guide for Microsoft Word Exam MO-100

Published with the authorization of Microsoft Corporation by:
Pearson Education, Inc.

ISBN-13: 978-0-13-662804-0
ISBN-10: 0-13-662804-4

Library of Congress Control Number: 2020935470

1 2020

Trademarks
Microsoft and the trademarks listed at http://www.microsoft.com on the "Trademarks" webpage are trademarks of the Microsoft group of companies. All other marks are property of their respective owners.

Warning and Disclaimer
Every effort has been made to make this book as complete and as accurate as possible, but no warranty or fitness is implied. The information provided is on an "as is" basis. The author, the publisher, and Microsoft Corporation shall have neither liability nor responsibility to any person or entity with respect to any loss or damages arising from the information contained in this book or from the use of the programs accompanying it.

Special Sales
For information about buying this title in bulk quantities, or for special sales opportunities (which may include electronic versions; custom cover designs; and content particular to your business, training goals, marketing focus, or branding interests), please contact our corporate sales department at corpsales@pearsoned.com or (800) 382-3419.

For government sales inquiries, please contact governmentsales@pearsoned.com.

For questions about sales outside the U.S., please contact intlcs@pearson.com.

Editor-in-Chief
Brett Bartow

Executive Editor
Loretta Yates

Development Editor
Songlin Qiu

Sponsoring Editor
Charvi Arora

Managing Editor
Sandra Schroeder

Senior Project Editor
Tracey Croom

Copy Editor
Elizabeth Welch

Indexer
Cheryl Ann Lender

Proofreader
Abigail Manheim

Technical Editor
Boyd Nolan

Editorial Assistant
Cindy Teeters

Cover Designer
Twist Creative, Seattle

Compositor
codeMantra

Contents

Introduction

The Microsoft Office Specialist (MOS) certification program has been designed to validate your knowledge of and ability to use applications in the Microsoft Office suite. This book has been designed to guide you in studying the types of tasks you are likely to be required to demonstrate in Exam MO-100: Microsoft Word 2019.

See Also For information about the tasks you are likely to be required to demonstrate in Exam MO-100: Microsoft Word (Word and Word 2019) Expert, see *MOS Study Guide for Microsoft Word Expert Exam MO-101* by Paul McFedries (Microsoft Press, 2020).

Who this book is for

MOS Study Guide for Microsoft Word Exam MO-100 is designed for experienced computer users seeking Microsoft Office Specialist certification in Word 2019 or the equivalent version of Word for Office 365.

MOS exams for individual programs are practical rather than theoretical. You must demonstrate that you can complete certain tasks or projects rather than simply answer questions about program features. The successful MOS certification candidate will have at least six months of experience using all aspects of the application on a regular basis; for example, using Word at work or school to create and manage documents, format document content, present information in tables and lists, insert and format pictures, create business diagrams, and reference information sources.

As a certification candidate, you probably have a lot of experience with the program you want to become certified in. Many of the procedures described in this book will be familiar to you; others might not be. Read through each study section and ensure that you are familiar with the procedures, concepts, and tools discussed. In some cases, images depict the tools you will use to perform procedures related to the skill set. Study the images and ensure that you are familiar with the options available for each tool.

How this book is organized

The exam coverage is divided into chapters representing broad skill sets that correlate to the functional groups covered by the exam. Each chapter is divided into sections addressing groups of related skills that correlate to the exam objectives. Each section includes review information, generic procedures, and practice tasks you can complete on your own while studying. We provide practice files you can use to work through the practice tasks, and results files you can use to check your work. You can practice the generic procedures in this book by using the practice files supplied or by using your own files.

Throughout this book, you will find Exam Strategy tips that present information about the scope of study that is necessary to ensure that you achieve mastery of a skill set and are successful in your certification effort.

Download the practice files

Before you can complete the practice tasks in this book, you need to copy the book's practice files and results files to your computer. Download the compressed (zipped) folder from the following page, and extract the files from it to a folder (such as your Documents folder) on your computer:

https://MicrosoftPressStore.com/MOSWord100/downloads

IMPORTANT The Word 2019 program is not available from this website. You should purchase and install that program before using this book.

You will save the completed versions of practice files that you modify while working through the practice tasks in this book. If you later want to repeat the practice tasks, you can download the original practice files again.

The following table lists the practice files provided for this book.

Folder and objective group	Practice files	Result files
MOSWord2019\Objective1 Manage documents	Word_1-1.docx Word_1-2.docx Word_1-3.docx Word_1-4.docx	Word_1-1_results.docx Word_1-2_results.docx Word_1-3_results.docx MyCompatible.doc Word_1-4_results.docx
MOSWord2019\Objective2 Insert and format text, paragraphs, and sections	Word_2-1.docx Word_2-2.docx Word_2-3.docx	Word_2-1_results.docx Word_2-2_results.docx Word_2-3_results.docx
MOSWord2019\Objective3 Manage tables and lists	Word_3-1.docx Word_3-2.docx Word_3-3.docx	Word_3-1_results.docx Word_3-2_results.docx Word_3-3_results.docx
MOSWord2019\Objective4 Create and manage references	Word_4-1.docx Word_4-2a.docx Word_4-2b.docx Word_4-2c.docx	Word_4-1_results.docx Word_4-2a_results.docx Word_4-2b_results.docx Word_4-2c_results.docx
MOSWord2019\Objective5 Insert and format graphic elements	Word_5-1.docx Word_5-1.glb Word_5-1.jpg Word_5-2.docx Word_5-3.docx Word_5-4.docx	Word_5-1_results.docx Word_5-2_results.docx Word_5-3_results.docx Word_5-4_results.docx
MOSWord2019\Objective6 Manage document collaboration	Word_6-1.docx Word_6-2.docx	Word_6-1_results.docx Word_6-2_results.docx

Adapt procedure steps

This book contains many images of user interface elements that you'll work with while performing tasks in Word on a Windows computer. Depending on your screen resolution or app window width, the Word ribbon on your screen might look different from that shown in this book. (If you turn on Touch mode, the ribbon displays significantly fewer commands than in Mouse mode.) As a result, procedural instructions that involve the ribbon might require a little adaptation.

Simple procedural instructions use this format:

➜ On the **Insert** tab, in the **Illustrations** group, click the **Chart** button.

If the command is in a list, our instructions use this format:

➜ On the **Home** tab, in the **Editing** group, click the **Find** arrow and then, in the **Find** list, click **Go To**.

If differences between your display settings and ours cause a button to appear differently on your screen than it does in this book, you can easily adapt the steps to locate the command. First click the specified tab, and then locate the specified group. If a group has been collapsed into a group list or under a group button, click the list or button to display the group's commands. If you can't immediately identify the button you want, point to likely candidates to display their names in ScreenTips.

The instructions in this book assume that you're interacting with on-screen elements on your computer by clicking (with a mouse, touchpad, or other hardware device). If you're using a different method—for example, if your computer has a touchscreen interface and you're tapping the screen (with your finger or a stylus)—substitute the applicable tapping action when you interact with a user interface element.

Instructions in this book refer to user interface elements that you click or tap on the screen as *buttons*, and to physical buttons that you press on a keyboard as *keys*, to conform to the standard terminology used in documentation for these products.

Ebook edition

If you're reading the ebook edition of this book, you can do the following:

- Search the full text
- Print
- Copy and paste

You can purchase and download the ebook edition from the Microsoft Press Store at:

https://MicrosoftPressStore.com/MOSWord100/detail

Errata, updates, & book support

We've made every effort to ensure the accuracy of this book and its companion content. If you discover an error, please submit it to us through the link at:

https://MicrosoftPressStore.com/MOSWord100/errata

For additional book support and information, please visit:

https://MicrosoftPressStore.com/Support

Please note that product support for Microsoft software and hardware is not offered through the previous addresses. For help with Microsoft software or hardware, visit:

https://support.microsoft.com

Stay in touch

Let's keep the conversation going! We're on Twitter at:

https://twitter.com/MicrosoftPress

Taking a Microsoft Office Specialist exam

Desktop computing proficiency is increasingly important in today's business world. When screening, hiring, and training employees, employers can feel reassured by relying on the objectivity and consistency of technology certification to ensure the competence of their workforce. As an employee or job seeker, you can use technology certification to prove that you already have the skills you need to succeed, saving current and future employers the time and expense of training you.

Microsoft Office Specialist certification

Microsoft Office Specialist certification is designed to assist students and information workers in validating their skills with Office programs. The following certification paths are available:

- A Microsoft Office Specialist is an individual who has demonstrated proficiency by passing the Excel Associate, Word Associate, Outlook Associate, or Power-Point Associate certification exam.

- A Microsoft Office Specialist Associate (MOS Associate) is an individual who has passed any three of the Associate-level certification exams.

- A Microsoft Office Specialist Expert (MOS Expert) is an individual who has completed the MOS Associate credential and any two of the three Expert-level exams: Access Expert, Word Expert, or Excel Expert.

Selecting a certification path

When deciding which certifications you would like to pursue, assess the following:

- The program and program version(s) with which you are familiar

- The length of time you have used the program and how frequently you use it

- Whether you have had formal or informal training in the use of that program

- Whether you use most or all of the available program features
- Whether you are considered a go-to resource by business associates, friends, and family members who have difficulty with the program

Candidates for MOS Associate certification are expected to successfully complete a wide range of standard business tasks. Successful candidates generally have six or more months of experience with the specific Office program, including either formal, instructor-led training or self-study using MOS-approved books, guides, or interactive computer-based materials.

Candidates for MOS Expert certification are expected to successfully complete more complex tasks that involve using the advanced functionality of the program. Successful candidates generally have at least six months, and might have several years, of experience with the programs, including formal, instructor-led training or self-study using MOS-approved materials.

Test-taking tips

Every MOS certification exam is developed from a set of exam skill standards (referred to as the *objective domain*) that are derived from studies of how the Office programs are used in the workplace. Because these skill standards dictate the scope of each exam, they provide critical information about how to prepare for certification. This book follows the structure of the published exam objectives.

See Also For more information about the book structure, see "How this book is organized" in the Introduction.

The MOS certification exams are performance based and require you to complete business-related tasks in the program for which you are seeking certification. For example, you might be presented with a document and told to insert and format additional document elements. Your score on the exam reflects how many of the requested tasks you complete within the allotted time.

Here is some helpful information about taking the exam:

- Keep track of the time. Your exam time does not officially begin until after you finish reading the instructions provided at the beginning of the exam. During the exam, the amount of time remaining is shown in the exam instruction window. You can't pause the exam after you start it.

- Pace yourself. At the beginning of the exam, you will receive information about the tasks that are included in the exam. During the exam, the number of completed and remaining tasks is shown in the exam instruction window.

- Read the exam instructions carefully before beginning. Follow all the instructions provided completely and accurately.

- If you have difficulty performing a task, you can restart it without affecting the result of any completed tasks, or you can skip the task and come back to it after you finish the other tasks on the exam.

- Enter requested information as it appears in the instructions, but without duplicating the formatting unless you are specifically instructed to do so. For example, the text and values you are asked to enter might appear in the instructions in bold and underlined text, but you should enter the information without applying these formats.

- Close all dialog boxes before proceeding to the next exam item unless you are specifically instructed not to do so.

- Don't close task panes before proceeding to the next exam item unless you are specifically instructed to do so.

- If you are asked to print a document, worksheet, chart, report, or slide, perform the task, but be aware that nothing will actually print.

- Don't worry about extra keystrokes or mouse clicks. Your work is scored based on its result, not on the method you use to achieve that result (unless a specific method is indicated in the instructions).

- If a computer problem occurs during the exam (for example, if the exam does not respond or the mouse no longer functions) or if a power outage occurs, contact a testing center administrator immediately. The administrator will restart the computer and return the exam to the point where the interruption occurred, with your score intact.

Exam Strategy This book includes special tips for effectively studying for the Microsoft Office Specialist exams in Exam Strategy paragraphs such as this one.

Certification benefits

At the conclusion of the exam, you will receive a score report, indicating whether you passed the exam. If your score meets or exceeds the passing standard (the minimum required score), you will be contacted by email by the Microsoft Certification Program team. The email message you receive will include your Microsoft Certification ID and links to online resources, including the Microsoft Certified Professional site. On this site, you can download or order a printed certificate, create a virtual business card, order an ID card, review and share your certification transcript, access the Logo Builder, and access other useful and interesting resources, including special offers from Microsoft and affiliated companies.

Depending on the level of certification you achieve, you will qualify to display one of three logos on your business card and other personal promotional materials. These logos attest to the fact that you are proficient in the applications or cross-application skills necessary to achieve the certification. Using the Logo Builder, you can create a personalized certification logo that includes the MOS logo and the specific programs in which you have achieved certification. If you achieve MOS certification in multiple programs, you can include multiple certifications in one logo.

For more information

To learn more about the Microsoft Office Specialist exams and related courseware, visit:

www.certiport.com/mos

Microsoft Office Specialist

Exam MO-100

Microsoft Word 2019

This book covers the skills you need to have for certification as a Microsoft Office Specialist in Word 2019. Specifically, you need to be able to complete tasks that demonstrate the following skill sets:

1   Manage documents
2   Insert and format text, paragraphs, and sections
3   Manage tables and lists
4   Create and manage references
5   Insert and format graphic elements
6   Manage document collaboration

With these skills, you can create, populate, format the content of, and manage the types of documents most commonly used in a business environment.

Prerequisites

We assume that you have been working with Word 2019 for at least six months and that you know how to carry out fundamental tasks that are not specifically mentioned in the objectives for this Microsoft Office Specialist exam. Before you begin studying for this exam, you might want to make sure you are familiar with the information in this section.

Move around in a document

You can view various parts of the active document by using the vertical and horizontal scroll bars. Using the scroll bars does not move the cursor—it changes only the part of the document displayed in the window. For example, if you drag the vertical scroll box down to the bottom of the scroll bar, the end of the document comes into view, but the cursor stays in its original location.

Here are some other ways to use the scroll bars:

- Click the up or down scroll arrow on the vertical scroll bar to move the document window up or down one line of text.
- Click above or below the scroll box to move up or down one screen.
- Click the left or right scroll arrow on the horizontal scroll bar to move the document window to the left or right several characters at a time.
- Click to the left or right of the scroll box to move left or right one screen.

You can also move around in a document by moving the cursor. You can click to place the cursor at a particular location, or you can press a key or a key combination to move the cursor.

The following table shows the keys and key combinations you can use to move the cursor.

Pressing this key or key combination	Moves the cursor
Left Arrow	Left one character at a time
Right Arrow	Right one character at a time
Down Arrow	Down one line at a time

Pressing this key or key combination	Moves the cursor
Up Arrow	Up one line at a time
Ctrl+Left Arrow	Left one word at a time
Ctrl+Right Arrow	Right one word at a time
Home	To the beginning of the current line
End	To the end of the current line
Ctrl+Home	To the beginning of the document
Ctrl+End	To the end of the document
Ctrl+Page Up	To the beginning of the previous page
Ctrl+Page Down	To the beginning of the next page
Page Up	Up one screen
Page Down	Down one screen

Select text

Before you can edit or format text, you need to select it. You can select any amount of text by dragging through it. You can select specific units of text as follows:

- To select a word, double-click it. The word and the space following it are selected. Punctuation following a word is not selected.

- To select a sentence, click anywhere in the sentence while holding down the Ctrl key. The first character in the sentence through the space following the ending punctuation mark are selected.

- To select a paragraph, triple-click it. The paragraph and paragraph mark are selected.

You can select adjacent words, lines, or paragraphs by positioning the cursor at the beginning of the text you want to select, holding down the Shift key, and then pressing an arrow key or clicking at the end of the text that you want to select.

To select non-adjacent blocks of text, select the first block, hold down the Ctrl key, and then select the next block.

To select a block of text quickly, you can use the selection area—the empty area to the left of the document's text column. When the pointer is in the selection area, it changes from an I-beam to a right-pointing arrow. From the selection area, you can select specific units of text as follows:

- To select a line, click in the selection area to the left of the line.
- To select a paragraph, double-click in the selection area to the left of the paragraph.
- To select an entire document, triple-click anywhere in the selection area.

To deselect text, click anywhere in the document window other than the selection area.

Cut, copy, and paste content

Word offers several methods of cutting and copying content. After selecting the content, you can click buttons on the ribbon, use a keyboard shortcut, or right-click the selection and click commands on the shortcut menu. Cutting or copying content places it on the Microsoft Office Clipboard. You can paste content that is stored on the Clipboard into a document (or any Office file) by using commands from the ribbon, shortcut menu, or keyboard, or directly from the Clipboard.

Experienced users might find it fastest to use a keyboard shortcut. The main keyboard shortcuts for editing tasks are shown in the following table.

Task	Keyboard shortcut
Cut	Ctrl+X
Copy	Ctrl+C
Paste	Ctrl+V
Undo	Ctrl+Z
Repeat/Redo	Ctrl+Y

Exam Strategy When you paste content into a Word document, the Paste Options menu presents options for formatting the pasted content. Exam MO-100 does not include items that test your knowledge of the Paste Options menu.

You can move or copy text by dragging it within the same document. To copy the selection instead of moving it, hold down the Ctrl key while you drag. The dragged text is not stored on the Clipboard, but the Paste Options list is available when you release the mouse button so that you can adjust the formatting of the moved or copied content.

See Also For information about managing the Clipboard and pasting content in alternative formats, see "Objective 2.1: Insert text and paragraphs."

Access program commands and options

Commands for working with Word documents (rather than document content) are available from the Backstage view. You display the Backstage view by clicking the File tab on the ribbon.

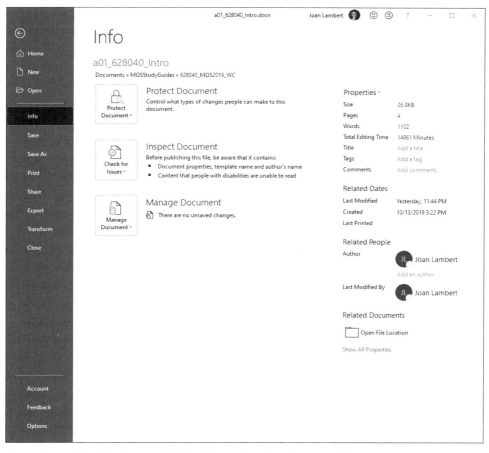

The Backstage view of a document displays information about the current document

The links in the left pane of the Backstage view provide access to information about the current document, commands for working with the document, or commands for working with Word. To display the Home, New, Open, Info, Save, Save As, Print, Share, Export, Transform, Account, or Feedback page, click the page name in the left pane.

You manage many aspects of Word functionality from the Word Options dialog box, which you open by clicking Options in the left pane of the Backstage view.

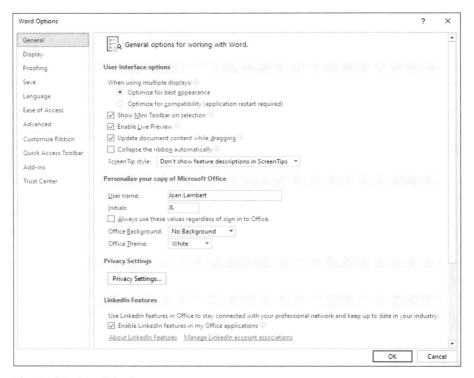

The Word Options dialog box

The Word Options dialog box has 11 separate pages of commands, organized by function. To display the General, Display, Proofing, Save, Language, Ease of Access, Advanced, Customize Ribbon, Customize Quick Access Toolbar, Add-ins, or Trust Center page of the Word Options dialog box, click the page name in the left pane.

Objective group 1

Manage documents

The skills tested in this section of the Microsoft Office Specialist exam for Microsoft Word 2019 relate to creating and managing documents. Specifically, the following objectives are associated with this set of skills:

- **1.1** Navigate within documents
- **1.2** Format documents
- **1.3** Save and share documents
- **1.4** Inspect documents for issues

You can modify the appearance of document content in Word to fit your needs and the needs of your audience, whether you're distributing the document in printed or electronic format. This chapter guides you in studying ways of navigating within documents and displaying hidden document content; formatting document content and page elements; saving, printing, and sharing documents; managing document properties; and locating and correcting issues related to privacy, accessibility, and compatibility.

To complete the practice tasks in this chapter, you need the practice files contained in the **MOSWord2019\Objective1** practice file folder. For more information, see "Download the practice files" in this book's introduction.

Objective 1.1: Navigate within documents

Word documents can include many elements to help readers locate the content they're looking for within long documents. The most important of these is a heading structure built by applying heading styles. Headings created in this way are visible in a structured format on the Headings tab of the Navigation pane.

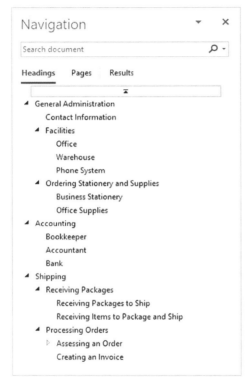

The Headings tab of the Navigation pane displays the document structure built by using heading styles

The Pages tab of the Navigation pane displays a thumbnail view of each page of the document. If you're looking for a specific element, such as an image or table, and don't know which section of the document it's in or a related search term that will take you to it, you can quickly scan the document content in this view.

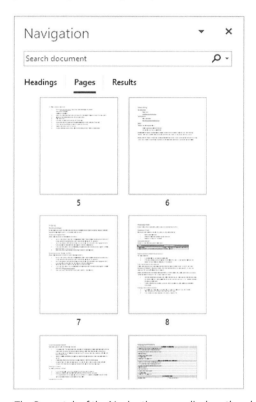

The Pages tab of the Navigation pane displays thumbnails of the document content

Search for text

If you're looking for a specific text phrase, you can search for it from the Navigation pane or from the Find tab of the Find And Replace dialog box. The Results tab of the Navigation pane displays the search results in context, whereas the Find tab locates only one instance of the search term at a time but allows you to define more search criteria.

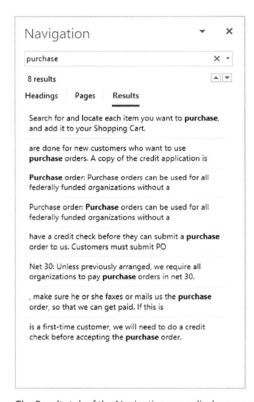

The Results tab of the Navigation pane displays search results in context

You can narrow the search results that are shown on the Results tab of the Navigation pane by specifying search parameters. The parameters available for a Navigation pane search are limited, but they are usually sufficient for defining searches that don't include wildcards, special characters, or formatting.

You can perform a more focused search from the Find And Replace dialog box, in which you can specify formatting options and include special characters in your search term.

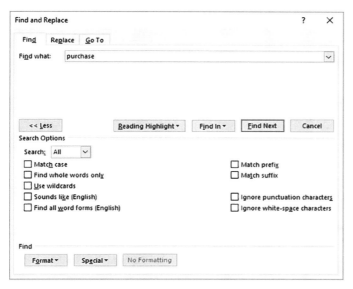

The Find And Replace dialog box expands to display additional search options

The following table identifies the characters available in the Special list.

Formatting marks and breaks	Wildcards	Special characters	Objects
Paragraph mark	Any character	Caret (^)	Field
Tab character	Any digit (numeric)	Section (§)	Graphic
Endnote mark		Paragraph (¶)	Nonbreaking hyphen
Footnote mark	Any letter	Em dash (—)	Nonbreaking space
Column break	White space	En dash (–)	Optional hyphen
Manual line break			
Manual page break			
Section break			

See Also For information about inserting page breaks, section breaks, and column breaks, see "Objective 2.3: Create and configure document sections."

To activate the Navigation pane search box

➜ Display the **Navigation** pane, and then click in the search box.

➜ Press **Ctrl+F**.

➜ On the **Home** tab, in the **Editing** group, click the **Find** button.

Tip The latter two options open the Navigation pane, if it isn't already open.

To locate specific text

1. In the **Navigation** pane search box, enter a search term (words, characters, and caret codes) in the search box to highlight all occurrences of the search term in the document and display them on the Results tab of the Navigation pane.

2. Display the **Results** tab of the **Navigation** pane, and then do any of the following:

   - Review the search results in context to locate a specific result.

   - Point to a search result to display the number of the page on which it appears and the heading that precedes it.

   - Click a search result to move to that location in the document.

   - Click the **Previous** or **Next** button to move among the search results.

   - Click the **End your search** button (the **X**) at the right end of the search box to clear the search results.

To restrict text search results from the Navigation pane

1. In the **Navigation** pane, click the **Search for more things** arrow at the right end of the search box, and then click **Options**.

2. In the **Find Options** dialog box, select the search criteria you want, and then click **OK**.

Tip Selecting an option in the Find Options dialog box clears the current search criteria from the search box at the top of the Navigation pane.

```
Find Options                                          ?    ×

  ☐ Match case            ☐ Match prefix
  ☐ Find whole words only ☐ Match suffix
  ☐ Use wildcards         ☐ Ignore punctuation characters
  ☐ Sounds like (English) ☐ Ignore white-space characters
  ☐ Find all word forms (English)
  ☑ Highlight all
  ☑ Incremental find



  Set As Default                        OK          Cancel
```

Options for searching from the Navigation pane

3. Enter the search term in the **Search** box.

To display the Find tab of the Find And Replace dialog box

→ In the **Navigation** pane, click the **Search for more things** arrow at the right end of the search box, and then click **Advanced Find**.

→ On the **Home** tab, in the **Editing** group, click the **Find** arrow, and then click **Advanced Find**.

→ Press **Ctrl+G**, and then click the **Find** tab.

Link to locations within documents

Word documents can include hyperlinks that provide a quick way to perform tasks such as the following:

- Link to a location within a document.
- Open another document.
- Link to a website.
- Download a file.
- Send an email message.

You can configure each hyperlink to display a unique ScreenTip.

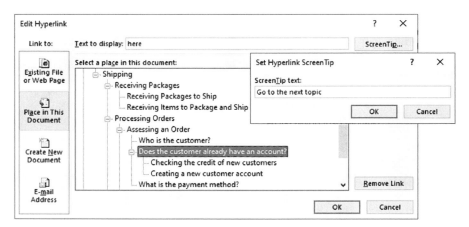

You can specify the display of a descriptive ScreenTip for each hyperlink

Exam Strategy Exam MO-100: Microsoft Word Associate requires that you demonstrate the ability to link to locations within a document. You do not need to demonstrate linking to websites or external files or sending email messages.

Within a document, hyperlinks appear underlined and in the Hyperlink color speci-fied by the document color scheme. You can jump to the target of the hyperlink by holding down the Ctrl key and clicking the link. After you click the hyperlink, its color changes to the Followed Hyperlink color specified by the color scheme.

When linking to content in the same document, document headings created by using heading styles are automatically available in the list of places within the document. If you want to link to content other than headings, you can insert named bookmarks to identify the content, and then link to the bookmark.

You can use whatever naming convention you like, provided it doesn't include spaces.

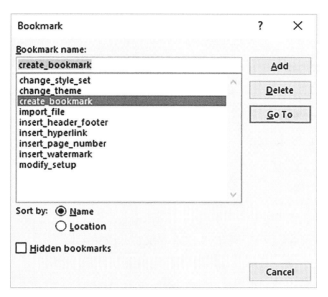

Link to any location within a document by inserting and linking to a bookmark

See Also For information about navigation to bookmarks, see "Move to specific locations and objects in documents" later in this section.

Bookmarks are available from the Bookmark dialog box, on the Go To page of the Find And Replace dialog box, and in the Select A Place In This Document list in the Insert Hyperlink dialog box. You can move to bookmarked locations within a document either by creating hyperlinks to the bookmarks or by navigating to them.

To open the Insert Hyperlink dialog box

➜ Do any of the following:

- On the **Insert** tab, in the **Links** group, click the **Add a Hyperlink** button.
- Right-click the selection, and then click **Hyperlink**.
- Press **Ctrl+K**.

To insert a hyperlink to a heading or bookmark within the document

1. Select the text or graphic object to which you want to attach the hyperlink, and then open the **Insert Hyperlink** dialog box.

Tip You can change the selected text from within the Insert Hyperlink dialog box by changing it in the Text To Display box.

2. On the **Link to** bar, click the **Place in This Document** button.

3. In the **Select a place in this document** box, click the heading or bookmark you want to link to.

4. In the **Insert Hyperlink** dialog box, click **OK**.

To specify ScreenTip text for a hyperlink

1. In the upper-right corner of the **Edit Hyperlink** dialog box, click the **ScreenTip** button.

2. In the **Set Hyperlink ScreenTip** dialog box, enter the text you want Word to display when a reader points to the hyperlink. Then click **OK**.

Tip The maximum length for a hyperlink ScreenTip is 256 characters, including spaces and punctuation. However, it's always nice to be concise!

To modify a hyperlink

1. Right-click the hyperlink, and then click **Edit Hyperlink**.

2. In the **Edit Hyperlink** dialog box, make the necessary changes, and then click **OK**.

To remove a hyperlink

➜ Right-click the hyperlink, and then click **Remove Hyperlink**.

To insert a bookmark

1. Place the cursor at the location in which you want to insert the bookmark, or select the text or object to which you want to attach the bookmark.

2. On the **Insert** tab, in the **Links** group, click the **Bookmark** button.

3. In the **Bookmark** dialog box, enter a name for the bookmark in the **Bookmark name** box, and then click **Add**.

Tip Bookmark names cannot contain spaces. If you include a space, the Add button becomes inactive. To name bookmarks with multiple words, either use internal capitalization or replace the spaces with underscores for readability.

To move to a bookmark

1. Open the **Bookmark** dialog box, and then click the bookmark you want to move to.

2. Do either of the following:

   - Click **Go To**, and then click **Close**.

   - On the **Home** tab, in the **Editing** group, click **Go To** in the **Find** list.

3. On the **Go To** page of the **Find and Replace** dialog box, in the **Go to what** list, click **Bookmark**.

4. In the **Enter bookmark name** list, click the bookmark you want.

5. Click **Go To**, and then click **Close**.

Move to specific locations and objects in documents

From the Go To tab of the Find And Replace dialog box, you can quickly move between pages, sections, lines, bookmarks, comments, footnotes, endnotes, fields, tables, graphics, equations, objects, or headings in a document.

Use the Go To feature to move to a specific type of element within a document

To locate specific objects

→ In the **Navigation** pane, click the **Search for more things** arrow at the right end of the search box, and then do either of the following:

- Click **Graphics**, **Tables**, **Equations**, **Footnotes/Endnotes**, or **Comments** to highlight all instances of the item in the document, highlight the document sections that contain the item on the Headings page of the Navigation pane, and display the specific results on the Pages page of the Navigation pane.

- Click **Go To**. On the **Go To** tab of the **Find and Replace** dialog box, click the type of object you want to locate, and then click the **Previous** or **Next** button.

To locate text and special characters from the Find And Replace dialog box

1. Display the **Find** tab of the **Find and Replace** dialog box.

2. Click **More** in the lower-left corner of the dialog box to display additional search options.

3. In the **Find what** box, enter the text you want to locate. If you want to include a special character or wildcard in your search term, click the **Special** button, and then click the item you want to locate to insert its caret code into the Find What box.

4. Modify your search by selecting any of the following options in the expanded dialog box:

- Guide the direction of the search by selecting **Down**, **Up**, or **All** from the **Search** list.

- Locate only text that matches the capitalization of the search term by selecting the **Match case** check box.

- Exclude occurrences of the search term that appear within other words by selecting the **Find whole words only** check box.

- Find two similar words, such as *effect* and *affect*, by selecting the **Use wildcards** check box and then including one or more wildcard characters in the search term.

Tip The two most common wildcard characters are ?, which represents any single character in the given location, and *, which represents any number of characters in the given location. For a list of the available wildcards, select the Use Wildcards check box and then click the Special button.

1

- Find occurrences of the search text that sound the same but are spelled differently, such as *there* and *their*, by selecting the **Sounds like** check box.
- Find occurrences of a particular word in any form, such as *try*, *tries*, and *tried*, by selecting the **Find all word forms** check box.
- Locate formatting or styles by selecting them from the **Format** list.
- Locate words with the same beginning or end as the search term by selecting the **Match prefix** or **Match suffix** check box.
- Locate words with different hyphenation or spacing by selecting the **Ignore punctuation characters** or **Ignore white-space characters** check box.

5. Click the **Find** button to locate the first instance of the search term.

To use the Go To function to find elements within a document

1. Display the **Go To** tab of the **Find and Replace** dialog box by using one of the following methods:
   - On the **Home** tab, in the **Editing** group, click the **Find** arrow, and then click **Go To**.
   - Press **Ctrl+G**.

2. In the **Go to what** list, click the type of element you want to locate.

3. Do either of the following:
   - In the **Enter *element*** box, select or enter the identifier of the specific element you want to locate. Then to move to that element, click **Go To**.
   - Click the **Next** or **Previous** button to move among instances of the selected element in the document.

Show or hide formatting symbols and hidden text

When you are fine-tuning the layout of a document, you might find it helpful to display formatting marks and hidden characters. Formatting marks, such as tabs, paragraph marks, page breaks, and section breaks, control the layout of your document, and hidden characters provide the structure for behind-the-scenes processes, such as indexing.

To display or hide formatting marks and hidden characters

→ On the **Home** tab, in the **Paragraph** group, click the **Show/Hide ¶** button.

→ Press **Ctrl+Shift+8** (**Ctrl+***).

Objective 1.1 practice tasks

The practice file for these tasks is in the **MOSWord2019\Objective1** practice file folder. The folder also contains a result file that you can use to check your work.

➤ Open the **Word_1-1** document, and then do the following:

- ❑ From the Navigation pane, locate all instances of **to**.

- ❑ Review the search results on the *Results* tab of the Navigation pane.

- ❑ Modify the search term to locate all instances of **toy**. Move between the search results by using the navigation buttons on the *Results* tab.

- ❑ Modify the search options to locate only instances of the capitalized word **Toymakers**, and then review the results.

- ❑ Perform an advanced search for all instances of **Toy** or **toy**, either capitalized or lowercase, that have the *Heading 2* style applied.

➤ Display the Contact Us section of the document, and then do the following:

- ❑ Select the name *Lola Jacobsen* and insert a bookmark named **SalesManager**.

- ❑ Attach a bookmark named **DesignManager** to the name *Sarah Jones*.

- ❑ Note the brackets around the names that indicate that they are bookmarks.

➤ Display the table of contents, and then do the following:

- ❑ Insert a hyperlink from each of the six first-level headings in the table of contents to the corresponding heading in the document.

➤ Return to the beginning of the document, and then use the Go To function to do the following:

❑ Move between graphics in the document until you reach the end.

❑ Move from the last graphic to the top of page 3.

❑ Move from the top of page 3 to the *SalesManager* bookmark.

➤ Save the **Word_1-1** document. Open the **Word_1-1_results** document and compare the two documents to check your work. Then close the open documents.

Objective 1.2: Format documents

Modify page setup

You control the layout of the pages in a document by changing the following three elements:

- **Paper size** You can select a standard paper size or enter custom dimensions.
- **Orientation** You can switch the direction in which a page is laid out on the paper. The default orientation is Portrait, in which the page is taller than it is wide. You can set the orientation to Landscape, in which the page is wider than it is tall.
- **Margins** Changing the margins of a document changes where information can appear on each page. You can select one of Word's predefined sets of top, bottom, left, and right margins, or set custom margins.

All the pages of a document have the same paper size, orientation, and margins unless you divide the document into sections. Then each section can have independent orientation and margin settings.

See Also For more information about sections, see "Objective 2.3: Create and configure document sections."

You can select standard configurations for these elements from the Layout tab of the ribbon. You can configure nonstandard options from the Page Setup dialog box.

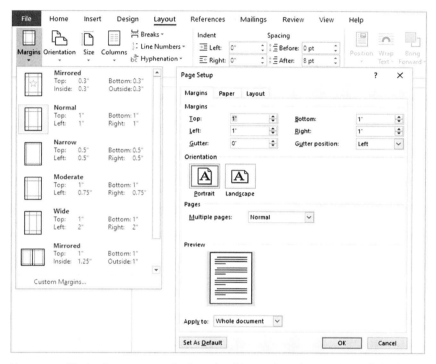

You can modify the document margins from the ribbon or from the Page Setup dialog box

The commands in the Page Setup dialog box are divided among three tabs: Margins, Paper, and Layout.

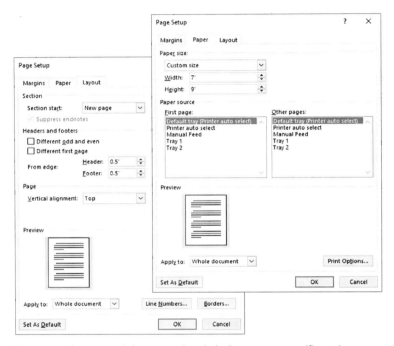

You can apply structural changes to the whole document or specific sections

To open the Page Setup dialog box

→ On the **Layout** tab, in the **Page Setup** group, do any of the following:

- Click the **Page Setup** dialog box launcher.
- Click the **Margins** button, and then click **Custom Margins**.
- Click the **Size** button, and then click **More Paper Sizes**.

To change the page margins

→ On the **Layout** tab, in the **Page Setup** group, click the **Margins** button, and then click the standard margin set you want.

Or

1. Open the **Page Setup** dialog box.

2. On the **Margins** tab of the **Page Setup** dialog box, specify the individual margins, the gutter width and position, the configuration of multiple pages, and the area of the document to which you want to apply the custom margins. Then click **OK**.

To change the page orientation

➜ On the **Layout** tab, in the **Page Setup** group, click the **Orientation** button, and then click **Portrait** or **Landscape**.

➜ On the **Margins** tab of the **Page Setup** dialog box, in the **Orientation** section, click the **Portrait** or **Landscape** thumbnail. Then click **OK**.

To change the page size

➜ On the **Layout** tab, in the **Page Setup** group, click the **Size** button, and then click the standard page size you want.

Or

1. On the **Size** menu, click **More Paper Sizes**.

2. On the **Paper** tab of the **Page Setup** dialog box, select **Custom size** in the **Paper size** list, define the width and height of the page, and then click **OK**.

Apply style sets

You can easily change the appearance and outline level of words and paragraphs by using styles. Styles can include character formatting, paragraph formatting, or a combination of both. Styles are stored in the template that is attached to a document. Styles are usually built on a base style (such as the Normal style) and use the default body font, heading font, and color set associated with the document's theme. For this reason, formatting document text and graphics by using styles produces a harmonious effect.

See Also For information about applying character styles and paragraph styles, see "Objective 2.2: Format text and paragraphs."

The appearance of content that is formatted by using styles is controlled by *style sets*. After you apply styles to document content, you can easily change the look of the entire document by switching to a different style set, which associates different formatting rules with the same styles.

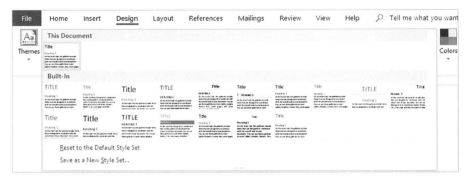

Pointing to a style set temporarily displays a live preview of the effect of applying it to your document

To apply a style set

→ On the **Design** tab, in the **Document Formatting** gallery, click the style set you want to apply.

To reset the style set to the template default

→ On the **Design** tab, expand the **Document Formatting** gallery, and then on the **Document Formatting** menu, click **Reset to the *template* Style Set**.

Exam Strategy   The objective domain for Exam MO-100 includes coverage of applying existing style sets to documents. Creating and modifying custom style sets is part of the objective domain for Exam MO-101, "Microsoft Word 2019 Expert."

Insert and modify headers and footers

You can display information on every page of your document by creating headers and footers. You can populate and format headers and footers independently. You can have a different header and footer on the first page of a document, different headers and footers on odd and even pages, or different headers and footers for each section.

You can manually insert text or graphic elements in a header or footer, select common elements (such as page number, date and time, or a document property) from a menu, or insert a preformatted building block.

When the header or footer is active for editing, Word displays a dashed border between the header or footer and the document body, and the Design tool tab appears on the ribbon. You can enter information in the header and footer areas the same way you enter ordinary text. You can also use the commands on the Design tool tab to enter and format document information, move from one header or footer to another, and establish the location and position of the header and footer.

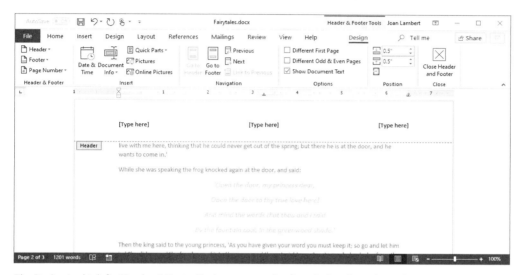

The Design tool tab for Header & Footer Tools appears only when the header or footer is active

---

Tip If your document contains section breaks, each successive section inherits the headers and footers of the preceding section unless you break the link between the two sections. After you break the link, you can create a different header and footer for the current section.

You can manually insert a page number element in a header or footer, or you can use the separate Page Number feature to insert stylized page numbers.

See Also For more information about inserting preformatted page numbers, see "Insert page numbers" later in this section.

To activate the header or footer

→ Do either of the following:

- Position the cursor anywhere in the document. On the **Insert** tab, in the **Header & Footer** group, click the **Header** button or the **Footer** button, and then click the corresponding **Edit** command on the menu.

- In Print Layout view, double-click in the top margin of a page to activate the header or in the bottom margin to activate the footer.

To insert custom header or footer content

1. Activate the header or footer.

2. In the header or footer area, do any of the following:

- Insert and format content by using the standard commands.

- From the **Insert** group on the **Design** tool tab, insert the date, time, an image, document information, or any Quick Parts you want to include.

- Use the preset tabs to align content at the left margin, in the center, and at the right margin, or modify the tabs to meet your needs.

3. In the **Close** group, click the **Close Header and Footer** button.

To insert a preformatted header or footer

1. On the **Insert** tab, in the **Header & Footer** group, click the **Header** button or the **Footer** button.

2. In the **Header** gallery or the **Footer** gallery, click the design you want.

3. Replace any text placeholders and enter any other information you want to appear.

4. In the **Close** group, click the **Close Header and Footer** button.

Exam Strategy You can also insert predefined headers and footers from the Building Blocks Organizer that is available from the Text group on the Insert tab. However, it is not necessary that you demonstrate a working knowledge of the Building Blocks Organizer to pass Exam MO-100.

To insert the current date and/or time in a header or footer

1. Activate the header or footer, and then position the cursor where you want the date and/or time to appear.

2. On the **Design** tool tab, in the **Insert** group, click the **Insert Date and Time** button.

3. In the **Date and Time** dialog box, do the following, and then click **OK**:

   - Click the format in which you want the date and/or time to appear in the header or footer.

   - If you want Word to update the date and/or time in the header each time you save the document, select the **Update automatically** check box.

To modify standard header or footer settings

1. Activate the header or footer. Then on the **Design** tool tab, in the **Options** group, do any of the following:

   - Select the **Different First Page** check box if you want to use a different header or footer on the first page of the document. You might want to do this if, for example, the first page of the document is a cover page.

   - Select the **Different Odd & Even Pages** check box if you want to use different headers or footers for odd pages and for even pages. Select this option if the content of the header or footer is not centered and the document content will be viewed on facing pages.

   - Clear the **Show Document Text** check box if you find that you're distracted by the main document text when you're working in the header or footer.

2. In the **Position** group, set the **Header Position from Top** or **Footer Position from Bottom** distance.

3. In the **Close** group, click the **Close Header and Footer** button.

To delete a header or footer

→ Activate the header or footer. Press **Ctrl+A** to select all the content of the header or footer, and then press **Delete**.

→ On the **Insert** tab, in the **Header & Footer** group, click the **Header** or **Footer** button, and then click the corresponding **Remove** command.

Insert page numbers

It is quite common to insert page numbers in a document that will be printed. You can insert stylized page numbers in the header, footer, left margin or right margin, or at the current cursor position on each page. You can format the page numbers to follow a specific pattern.

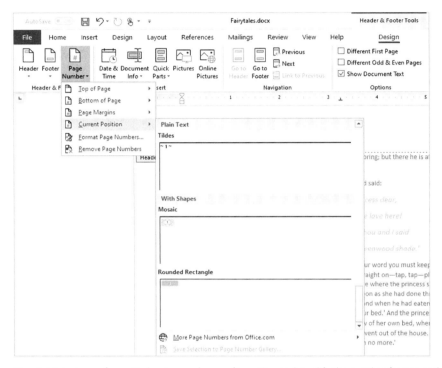

You can insert a preformatted page number configuration and modify the number format and separator

To insert a preformatted page number in a header or footer

1. On the **Insert** tab, in the **Header & Footer** group, click the **Page Number** button.

2. In the **Page Number** list, click the location at which you want to insert the page number, and then click the page number style you want.

To change the format of page numbers

1. On the **Insert** tab or **Design** tool tab (when the header or footer is active), in the **Header & Footer** group, click the **Page Number** button, and then click **Format Page Numbers**.

2. In the **Page Number Format** dialog box, in the **Number format** list, click the format you want.

3. Select any other options you want, and then click **OK**.

Format page background elements

You can modify the appearance of the page behind the document content by changing the page color, adding a simple or fancy page border, or displaying a watermark.

Enhance a document by adding page background elements

A watermark is a transparent word or phrase, or a muted graphic, that appears on the page background of a document but doesn't interfere with its readability. You can use a text watermark such as *Draft* or *Important* to indicate information about a document. You can use a graphic watermark to brand a document with your logo or to simply add flair.

Watermarks are visible when you display a document in Print Layout view or Web Layout view, and they are optional when printing a document.

To add a text watermark

1. On the **Design** tab, in the **Page Background** group, click **Watermark**.

2. In the **Watermark** gallery, click the thumbnail for one of the predefined text watermarks.

Or

1. On the **Watermark** menu, click **Custom Watermark**.

2. In the **Printed Watermark** dialog box, select **Text watermark**.

3. Either select the watermark text you want from the **Text** list, or enter the text in the **Text** box.

3. Format the text by changing the settings in the **Font**, **Size**, and **Color** boxes.

4. Choose a layout, select or clear the **Semitransparent** check box, and then click **OK**.

To use a picture as a watermark

1. On the **Watermark** menu, click **Custom Watermark**.

2. In the **Printed Watermark** dialog box, select **Picture watermark**, and then click the **Select Picture** button.

3. In the **From a file** area of the **Insert Pictures** dialog box, click **Browse**. In the **Insert Picture** dialog box that opens, navigate to the folder where the picture is stored, and double-click the picture file to insert the file path in the **Printed Watermark** dialog box.

4. In the **Scale** list, choose how big or small you want the watermark picture to appear in the document.

5. If you want to display a more vibrant picture, clear the **Washout** check box. Then click **OK**.

To change the page background color

1. On the **Design** tab, in the **Page Background** group, click **Page Color**.

2. On the **Page Color** menu, do one of the following:

   - Select a color from the **Theme Colors** or **Standard Colors** palette.
   - Select **More Colors**, select a standard color or enter a custom color code, and then click **OK**.

To specify a page border

1. On the **Design** tab, in the **Page Background** group, click **Page Borders**.

2. On the **Page Border** tab of the **Borders and Shading** dialog box, select the type of border you want to apply. Then do either of the following:

   - Select the line style, color, and width.

   - Select a style from the **Art** list and then, if the **Color** option is available for the selected art, select a color.

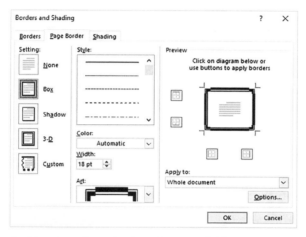

A wide variety of page border styles are available

3. By default, the border is applied to all four sides of each page of the whole document. If you want to change that, do either of the following:

   - In the **Preview** area, click a page border to remove it.

   - In the **Apply to** list, click the portion of the document to which you want to apply the page border.

4. Click **OK**.

Objective 1.2 practice tasks

The practice file for these tasks is in the **MOSWord2019\Objective1** practice file folder. The folder also contains a result file that you can use to check your work.

➤ Open the **Word_1-2** document, and then do the following:

❏ Set the document page color to *Tan, Background 2*.

❏ Configure a 1-point *Box* page border that uses a line style of your choice. (Do not use an Art style.)

❏ Add a diagonal watermark that displays the text **Example Only** to the page background. Format the text of the watermark as semitransparent 54-point *Lavender Accent 3* text. Apply the watermark and verify that it appears on all pages of the document.

❏ On page 2, add a *Sideline* header. Configure the header so that it does not appear on the first page of the document.

❏ On page 2, insert the *Circle, Right* page number in the right margin.

❏ Display the document title. Then apply the *Casual* style set to the document and note the resulting changes.

➤ Save the **Word_1-2** document. Open the **Word_1-2_results** document and compare the two documents to check your work. Then close the open documents.

Objective 1.3: Save and share documents

Modify basic document properties

In Word 2019, the properties of a document are easily accessible from the Info page of the Backstage view. You can view and modify some document properties directly on the Info page, or you can work in the Properties dialog box, which is available from within the document or from File Explorer.

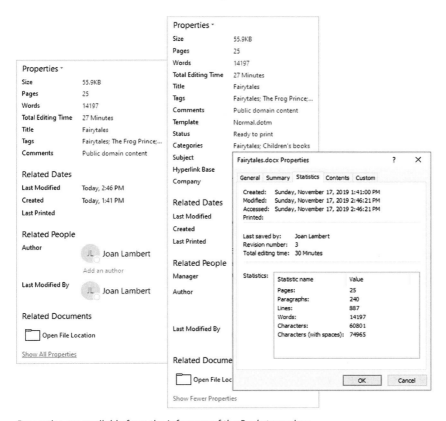

Properties are available from the Info page of the Backstage view

To set or change the Title, Tags, or Comments properties

➔ On the **Info** page of the Backstage view, click the property to activate it, and then add or change information.

To add an author to the Author property

→ On the **Info** page of the Backstage view, in the **Related People** area, click **Add an author**, and then do one of the following:

- Enter one or more author names or email addresses, separated by semicolons, and then click **Verify the contact names you have entered** to validate the entry against your organization's Global Address List and your other Microsoft Outlook address books.

Tip If Word finds a match for the author's name and you have that author's contact information stored in Outlook, you can initiate contact with that person from the Author list on the Info page.

- Click the **Search the Address Book for contacts** button. In the **Address Book** dialog box, select the address book in which the author's contact information is saved, and then select the author.

To remove an author from the Author property

→ On the **Info** page of the Backstage view, in the **Related People** area, right-click the author, and then click **Remove Person**.

To open the Properties dialog box

→ On the **Info** page of the Backstage view, click **Properties**, and then click **Advanced Properties**.

→ In File Explorer, right-click the file, and then click **Properties**.

Save documents in alternative file formats

The Office 2019 programs use file formats based on XML, called the *Microsoft Office Open XML Formats*, that were introduced with Office 2007. By default, Word 2019 files are saved in the .docx format, which is the Word variation of this file format.

The .docx format provides the following benefits:

- File size is smaller because files are compressed when saved, decreasing the amount of disk space needed to store the file and the amount of bandwidth needed to send files in email, over a network, or across the internet.

- Recovering at least some of the content of damaged files is possible because XML files can be opened in a text program such as Notepad.

- Security is greater because .docx files cannot contain macros, and personal data can be detected and removed from the file. (A different file format—.docm—is for documents that contain macros.)

In addition to these default Word 2019 formats, you can save a document that you create in Word 2019 in many other formats, including Word Macro-Enabled Document, Word Macro-Enabled Template, Word XML Document, Web Page, Word 97-2003 Template, Word 2003 XML Document, Strict Open XML Document, and Works 6-9 Document.

If you want to save a Word document in a format that can be opened by the widest variety of programs (including text editors that are installed with most operating systems), use one of these two formats:

- **Rich Text Format (.rtf)** This format preserves the document's formatting.
- **Plain Text (.txt)** This format preserves only the document's text.

If you want people to be able to view a document exactly as it appears on your screen, use one of these two formats:

- **PDF (.pdf)** This format is preferred by commercial printing facilities. Recipients can display the file in the free Microsoft Reader or Adobe Reader programs, and can display and edit the file in Word 2019 or Adobe Acrobat.

- **XPS (.xps)** This format precisely renders all fonts, images, and colors. Recipients can display the file in the free Microsoft Reader program or the free XPS Viewer program.

The PDF and XPS formats are designed to deliver documents as electronic representations of the way they appear when printed. Both types of files can easily be sent by email to many recipients and can be made available on a webpage for downloading by anyone who wants them. However, the files are no longer Word documents. A PDF file can be converted to the editable Word format. An XPS file cannot be opened, viewed, or edited in Word.

When you save a Word document in PDF or XPS format, you can optimize the file size of the document for your intended distribution method—the larger Standard file size is better for printing, whereas the Minimum file size is suitable for online publishing. You can also configure the following options:

- Specify the pages to include in the PDF or XPS file.
- Include or exclude comments and tracked changes in a PDF file.
- Include or exclude nonprinting elements such as bookmarks and properties.
- Select compliance, font embedding, and encryption options in a PDF file.

To display the Save As dialog box

→ On the **Save As** page of the Backstage view, do any of the following:

- Below the **Places** list, click the **Browse** button.
- Above the file navigation controls, click the file path.
- Below the file navigation controls, click the **More options** link.

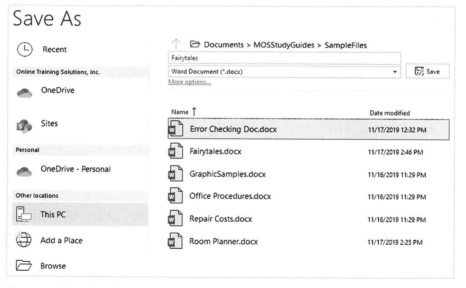

You can navigate through storage locations on the Save As page or in the Save As dialog box

→ On the **Export** page of the Backstage view, click **Change File Type**, click the file type you want, and then click **Save As**.

To save a file in an alternative file format with the default settings

➜ On the **Save As** page of the Backstage view, in the file type list at the top of the right column, click the format you want. Then click the **Save** button.

➜ In the **Save As** dialog box, in the **Save as type** list, click the format you want, and then click **Save**.

➜ On the **Export** page of the Backstage view, click **Change File Type**, click the file type you want, and click **Save As**. Then in the **Save As** dialog box that opens, click **Save**.

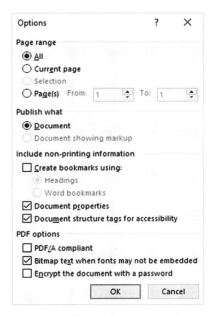

You can specify compliance standards when saving a document as a PDF file

To save a file in PDF or XPS format with custom settings

1. On the **Export** page of the Backstage view, click **Create PDF/XPS Document**, and then click the **Create PDF/XPS** button.

2. In the **Publish as PDF or XPS** dialog box, click **Options**.

3. In the **Options** dialog box, select the options you want for the PDF or XPS file, and then click **OK**.

Or

1. Open the **Save As** dialog box. In the **Save as type** list, click either **PDF** or **XPS Document**.

2. In the **Save As** dialog box, click **Options**.

3. In the **Options** dialog box, select the options you want for the PDF or XPS file, and then click **OK**.

<><><><><><><><><><><><><><><><><><><><><><><><><><><><><><><><><><><><><><><><>

Exam Strategy If Adobe Acrobat is installed on your computer, that program adds a custom Acrobat tab to the ribbon and a Save As Adobe PDF page to the Backstage view. When demonstrating the ability to perform tasks during the Microsoft Office Specialist exam, you can use only the functionality built into Word, which this book describes.

<><><><><><><><><><><><><><><><><><><><><><><><><><><><><><><><><><><><><><><><>

Modify print settings

When printing a document, you can specify what part of the document is printed and whether markup (tracked changes) is indicated in the printed document. In addition, you have the option of printing the following information instead of the document content:

- Document properties
- Tracked changes
- Styles
- AutoText entries
- Custom shortcut keys

In addition to these options, you can specify the following print settings:

- Print a multipage document on one or both sides of the paper. If your printer supports double-sided printing, you have the option of flipping the double-sided page on the long edge or the short edge (depending on how you plan to bind and turn the document pages).

- Print up to 16 pages on each sheet of paper. You can use this option to print a booklet with two pages per sheet that will be folded in the middle. You might also use this option to save paper when you're printing a long document, but bear in mind that as the number of pages per sheet increases, the size of the content printed on the page decreases.

- Print multiple copies of a document either with collated pages (all pages of each copy together) or uncollated pages (all copies of each page together).

- If your printer has multiple paper trays or a manual paper feeder, select the paper source you want to use.

Exam Strategy Some of the settings on the Print page of the Backstage view are dependent on the functionality supported by your printer. These settings might vary when you select a different device in the Printer list. The Microsoft Office Specialist exams don't require you to demonstrate the ability to use settings that are specific to physical printers.

Configure print settings and preview their effects

To select a printer

→ On the **Print** page of the Backstage view, in the **Printer** area, click the current printer, and then click the printer you want to use.

To print multiple copies of a document

→ On the **Print** page of the Backstage view, in the **Copies** box, click the arrows or enter the number of copies you want to print. If you want to print the copies of each page separately, click **Collated** in the **Settings** area, and then click **Uncollated**.

To print a specific portion of a document

→ On the **Print** page of the Backstage view, in the **Settings** area, click **Print All Pages** and then do any of the following:

- To print only the currently selected content, click **Print Selection**.

- To print only the page on which the cursor is active, click **Print Current Page**.

- To print specific pages or sections, click **Custom Print** and enter the pages, sections, or page ranges you want to print in the **Pages** box. Indicate page ranges by using a hyphen and multiple page selections by using a comma (for example, *1-3, 6* prints pages 1, 2, 3, and 6). Indicate sections and page ranges within sections by prefacing the page with *p* and the section with *s* (for example, *s2* prints the entire second section, and *p2s2-p4s2* prints pages 2–4 of the second section).

To print a document double-sided

→ On the **Print** page of the Backstage view, in the **Settings** area, click **Print One Sided** and then click the **Print on Both Sides** option that you want.

To print multiple pages on each sheet of paper

→ On the **Print** page of the Backstage view, in the **Settings** area, click **1 Page per Sheet** and then click the number of pages you want to print on each sheet.

To scale pages to a specific size

→ On the **Print** page of the Backstage view, in the **Settings** area, click **1 Page per Sheet**, click **Scale to Paper Size**, and then click the paper size to which you want to scale the sheets.

To specify a paper source

→ On the **Print** page of the Backstage view, in the **Settings** area, click the **Page Setup** link. On the **Paper** tab of the **Page Setup** dialog box, in the **Paper source** area, click the paper source you want. Then click **OK**.

Share documents electronically

As an alternative to distributing printed copies of a document, many people share documents electronically—by storing the document in a shared storage location or sending it in email.

Each personal or business Office 365 account includes Microsoft OneDrive online storage in which you can save and share documents (and access them yourself from anywhere, which is very useful in the event that you need something and are without your computer). By default, only you have access to the documents that you save to OneDrive. However, you can easily share a document or folder of documents with other people for the purpose of distributing or coauthoring a document.

The Microsoft Office suite also makes it easy to email documents from within Word—you don't even have to open your Outlook account to compose the message. If you're emailing a final document, Word offers the option of creating and sending a PDF version of the document with just one click.

These sharing options are available from the window that opens when you click Share in the left pane of the Backstage view.

You can share a document from a shared storage location or through email

To save a document to a shared storage location

1. In the left pane of the Backstage view, click **Share**.

2. In the **Share** window, click the OneDrive location to which you want to save the document.

OR

1. In the left pane of the Backstage view, click **Save As**.

2. If you've already connected Office to the shared storage location, select it in the location list, and then select a shared location to which you've already connected Office.

3. If you haven't yet connected to the shared storage location, follow these steps:

    In the **Other locations** list, click **Add a Place**.

    In the **Add a Place** list, select **OneDrive** to connect to a personal OneDrive storage folder or **OneDrive for Business** to connect to a corporate OneDrive storage folder.

    Enter your account credentials as prompted to complete the process.

To email the current document or a PDF version

1. In the left pane of the Backstage view, click **Share**.

2. In the **Share** window, select **Word Document** or **PDF**.

3. In the Outlook message window that opens, enter the recipient's name and any additional message content. Then click **Send**.

Objective 1.3 practice tasks

The practice file for these tasks is in the **MOSWord2019\Objective1** practice file folder. The folder also contains a result file that you can use to check your work.

➤ Open the **Word_1-3** document. Display the Backstage view, and then do the following:

❑ Set the *Title* property to **Simple Room Design** and the *Subject* property to **Room Planner**.

❑ Assign the keywords (tags) **color** and **style** to the document.

❑ Add yourself as the only author.

❑ Set the document *Status* to **Draft**.

➤ Save the **Word_1-3** document. Open the **Word_1-3_results** document and compare the two documents to check your work. Then do the following:

❑ Print the document using the Microsoft Print To PDF printer, with the scaling set to *2 Pages Per Sheet*.

❑ Save a copy of the document in the practice file folder as a file named **MyCompatible** that is compatible with Word 2002.

❑ If Outlook is installed on your computer, send a PDF copy of the **MyCompatible** Word document to yourself.

➤ Close the **MyCompatible** document.

Objective 1.4: Inspect documents for issues

Word includes three tools that you can use to inspect a document for possible problems before you distribute it electronically (as a file): the Document Inspector, the Accessibility Checker, and the Compatibility Checker.

The Document Inspector checks for content and information that you might not want to share with readers, such as:

- Information that identifies the document authors
- Tracked changes, comments, and ink annotations
- Content that is hidden or invisible
- Page headers, footers, and watermarks
- Macros, form controls, ActiveX controls, and embedded documents saved as part of the document or template
- Built-in and custom document properties
- Document version history, template name, and server properties

1

The Document Inspector offers to remove the content generating the issues that it locates but doesn't specifically identify that content within the document. You can opt to remove or retain any category of content. You might want to keep some types of content and review them individually.

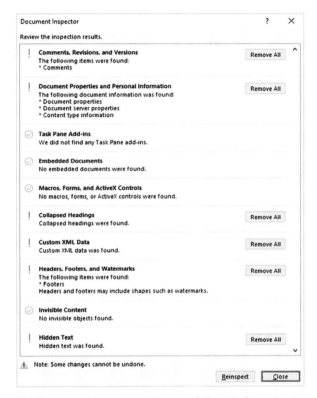

The Document Inspector provides pass/fail results for each category you choose

The Accessibility Checker identifies document elements and formatting that might be difficult for people with certain kinds of disabilities to read or for assistive devices such as screen readers to access. These issues are divided by decreasing severity into three classifications: Errors, Warnings, and Tips.

In Word documents, the Accessibility Checker inspects content to ensure that it meets the criteria shown in the following table.

Error rules	Warning rules	Tip rules
All nontext content has alternative text	Sufficient contrast between text and background	Layout tables are structured for easy navigation
Tables specify column header information		
Image or object is inline with text		Documents use heading styles
Document access is not restricted		

See Also For detailed information about Accessibility Checker rules, go to *support.office.com/ en-us/article/rules-for-the-accessibility-checker-651e08f2-0fc3-4e10-aaca-74b4a67101c1* (or go to *support.office.com* and search for "Accessibility Checker rules"). For more information about designing documents for accessibility, display the Accessibility Checker pane, and then click the Read More link at the bottom of the pane.

From the Accessibility Checker pane, you can select any issue to display information about why it might be a problem and how to fix it. You can leave the Accessibility Checker open while you work—its contents will automatically update to indicate the current issues.

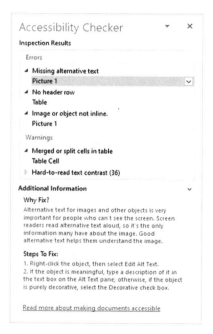

The Accessibility Checker pane provides links directly to possible issues

Tip After you run the Accessibility Checker, Word also displays information about document content issues in the Inspect Document area of the Info page of the Backstage view.

The Compatibility Checker identifies formatting and features that aren't supported or won't work as expected in Word 2010 and earlier versions. Fixing these issues ensures that the appearance and functionality of the document will be consistent for all readers.

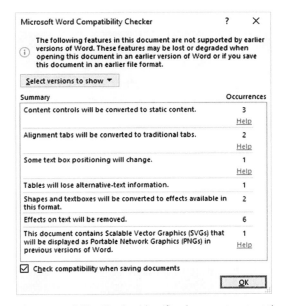

The Compatibility Checker identifies document content that will not display or function as expected in an earlier version of Word

The following table identifies Word 2019 document content features that aren't supported in earlier versions of Word.

Unsupported in Word 2010	Unsupported in Word 2007	Unsupported in Word 2003 and earlier
<ul><li>Headings that are collapsed by default</li><li>Threaded comments and comments marked as Done</li><li>Customized footnote columns</li><li>Web video</li><li>Apps for Office</li><li>Repeating section content controls and XML mappings on rich-text content controls</li></ul>	All features unsupported in Word 2010, and:<ul><li>Numbering formats, shapes, text boxes, and WordArt effects introduced in Word 2010 or later</li><li>Text effects</li><li>Alternative text assigned to tables</li><li>OpenType features</li><li>Blocking authors</li><li>Check box content controls</li></ul>	All features unsupported in Word 2007, and:<ul><li>Themes</li><li>Major/minor fonts</li><li>Tracked moves</li><li>Alignment tabs</li><li>SmartArt graphics</li><li>Office 2007 charts</li><li>Open XML Embedded objects</li><li>Building blocks and AutoText entries</li><li>Linked bibliographies and citations</li><li>Live equations</li><li>Relative positioning of text boxes</li></ul>

To locate and remove hidden properties and personal information

1. Save the document, and then display the **Info** page of the Backstage view.

2. In the **Inspect Document** area of the **Info** page, click the **Check for Issues** button, and then click **Inspect Document** to open the Document Inspector dialog box, which lists the items that will be checked.

3. Clear the check boxes for any groups of properties you don't want to check for, and then click **Inspect** to display a report on the presence of the properties you selected.

   In addition to the basic properties that are displayed in the Properties section of the Info page, the inspector might return information on headers and footers and custom XML data.

4. Review the results, and then click the **Remove All** button for any category of information that you want to remove.

Tip You can choose to retain content identified by the Document Inspector if you know that it is appropriate for distribution.

5. In the **Document Inspector** dialog box, click **Reinspect**, and then click **Inspect** to verify the removal of the properties and other data you selected.

6. When you're satisfied with the results, close the **Document Inspector** dialog box.

To locate and correct accessibility issues

1. On the **Info** page of the Backstage view, click the **Check For Issues** button, and then click **Check Accessibility** to run the Accessibility Checker.

2. In the **Accessibility Checker** pane, review the inspection results and make any changes you want to the document.

3. When you are done, do either of the following:

   • Click the **X** in the upper-right corner of the **Accessibility Checker** pane to close the pane.

   • Leave the pane open to continue checking for accessibility issues as you work with the document.

To locate and correct compatibility issues

1. On the **Info** page of the Backstage view, click the **Check for Issues** button, and then click **Check Compatibility**. The window immediately displays any formatting or features in the document that aren't compatible with Word 97–2003, Word 2007, or Word 2010.

2. To refine the list, click **Select versions to show** and then click **Word 97–2003**, **Word 2007**, or **Word 2010** to select or clear the version from the compatibility requirements. Selected versions are indicated by check marks preceding the version.

3. Review the issue description and note the number of instances of the issue within the document. Some issues include a Help link to additional information.

4. Locate the named element by searching or scanning the document, and then remove or modify it to meet the compatibility requirements.

5. When you finish, click **OK** to close the Compatibility Checker.

Objective 1.4 practice tasks

The practice file for these tasks is in the **MOSWord2019\Objective1** practice file folder. The folder also contains a result file that you can use to check your work.

➤ Open the **Word_1-4** document, review its content, and then do the following:

❑ Inspect the document for hidden properties or personal information.

❑ Remove the comments and hidden text located by the document inspector. Do not remove other issues that it identifies.

❑ Inspect the document for accessibility issues.

❑ From the Recommended Actions menus, mark *Picture 1* and *Picture 2* as decorative.

❑ From the Recommended Actions menu, display the *Box* in line with the text.

❑ Inspect the document for compatibility issues. Note the types of issues found by the inspector.

➤ Save the **Word_1-4** document. Open the **Word_1-4_results** document and compare the two documents to check your work. Then close the open documents.

Objective group 2

Insert and format text, paragraphs, and sections

The skills tested in this section of the Microsoft Office Specialist exam for Microsoft Word 2019 relate to formatting document content. Specifically, the following objectives are associated with this set of skills:

2.1   Insert text and paragraphs

2.2   Format text and paragraphs

2.3   Create and configure document sections

Word documents are merely containers for their content. You can create content directly in the document or reuse and adapt it from other sources. The way that you present the content—by formatting its appearance and structure and by maintaining consistency—can improve the effectiveness of the document in communicating a specific message.

This chapter guides you in studying ways of inserting text, symbols, and special characters; formatting text; modifying paragraph indentation, spacing, and layout; applying character and paragraph styles; and structuring a document by controlling page breaks, creating independently formatted sections, and formatting content in columns.

To complete the practice tasks in this chapter, you need the practice files contained in the **MOSWord2019\Objective2** practice file folder. For more information, see "Download the practice files" in this book's introduction.

Objective 2.1: Insert text and paragraphs

Replace text

See Also This topic is about replacing text through a find-and-replace operation. For information about locating specific text and objects or moving directly to specific types of objects, see "Objective 1.1: Navigate within documents."

When developing document content, you can ensure that the text in your documents is consistent and accurate by using the Find feature to review every occurrence of a specific word or phrase, or by using the Replace feature to consistently modify text, formatting, or styles. You can replace search terms with other text or special characters from the Replace tab of the Find And Replace dialog box.

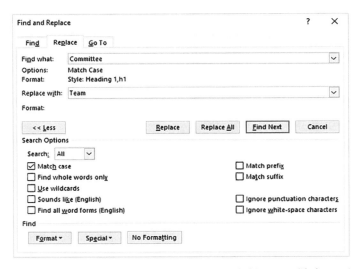

A Replace operation can replace or delete text and objects, modify formatting, and apply styles

To locate and replace text

1. Display the **Replace** page of the **Find and Replace** dialog box by doing any of the following:

   - In the **Navigation** pane, click the **Search for more things** arrow at the right end of the search box, and then click **Replace**.

   - On the **Home** tab, in the **Editing** group, click **Replace**.

   - Press **Ctrl+H**.

2. In the **Find what** box, specify the text or characters you want to locate by entering them directly or by selecting them from the **Special** list.

See Also For information about the Special list content, including formatting marks, breaks, wildcard characters, special characters, and objects, see "Objective 1.1: Navigate within documents."

3. In the **Search Options** area, select the check boxes of any applicable search options.

Tip The settings in the Search Options area apply only to the search term. They do not affect the replacement term.

4. With the cursor in the **Find what** box, from the **Format** list, select any formatting or styles that will specifically identify the correct search results.

5. In the **Replace with** box, enter the text or characters with which you want to replace the search term.

Tip You can't specify wildcard characters in the Replace With box. You can specify special characters. For example, you can use the Replace feature to remove blank paragraph marks from a document by replacing ^p^p (two paragraph marks) with ^p (one paragraph mark).

6. With the cursor in the **Replace with** box, from the **Format** list, select any formatting or styles that you want to apply as part of the replacement operation.

7. Click **Find Next** to find the first occurrence of the search term. Then do any of the following:

    -   Click **Find Next** to find the next occurrence of the search term.
    -   Click **Replace** to replace the selected occurrence with the text in the **Replace with** box and move to the next occurrence.
    -   Click **Replace All** to replace all occurrences of the search term in the document without individually reviewing them.

Tip You can quickly review all instances of a search term by searching from the Navigation pane and then scrolling through the search results on the Results page of the Navigation pane.

Insert symbols and special characters

Some documents require characters not found on a standard keyboard. These characters might include the copyright (©) or registered trademark (®) symbols, currency symbols (such as € or £), Greek letters, or letters with accent marks. Or you might want to add arrows (such as ↺ or ↿) or graphic icons (such as ⌨ or ♫). Word gives you easy access to a huge array of symbols that you can easily insert into any document. Like graphics, symbols can add visual information or eye appeal to a document. However, they are different from graphics in that they are keyboard characters displayed in specific fonts.

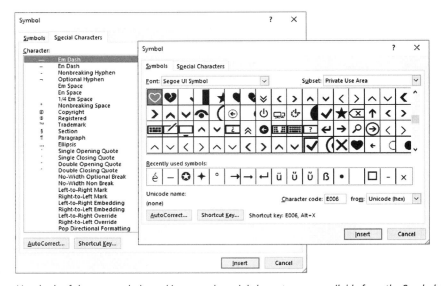

Hundreds of shapes, symbols, and icons, and special characters are available from the Symbol dialog box

---

Tip You can insert some common symbols by using keyboard shortcuts. You can review the assigned keyboard shortcuts in the Symbol dialog box and the AutoCorrect Options dialog box.

To insert a common symbol

→ On the **Insert** tab, in the **Symbols** group, click the **Symbol** button, and then click the symbol you want to insert.

→ Enter any of the following keyboard shortcuts:

- To insert a copyright symbol, enter **(c)** or press **Alt+Ctrl+C**.
- To insert a Euro symbol, enter **(e)**.
- To insert a registered trademark symbol, enter **(r)** or press **Alt+Ctrl+R**.
- To insert a trademark symbol, enter **(tm)** or press **Alt+Ctrl+T**.

Tip If you turn off the Replace Text As You Type option in the AutoCorrect settings, the paren-thetical code will not convert to the symbol.

To insert any symbol or special character

1. On the **Insert** tab, in the **Symbols** group, click the **Symbol** button, and then click **More Symbols**.

2. In the **Symbol** dialog box, do either of the following:

- On the **Special Characters** tab, double-click the character you want to insert.
- On the **Symbols** tab, locate and double-click the symbol you want to insert.

Tip The dialog box might be positioned in front of the cursor.

3. After you insert all the symbols you want, close the **Symbol** dialog box.

Objective 2.1 practice tasks

The practice file for these tasks is in the **MOSWord2019\Objective2** practice file folder. The folder also contains a result file that you can use to check your work.

➤ Open the **Word_2-1** document and do the following:

❑ In the first paragraph, insert the registered trademark symbol (®) after the word *Microsoft*.

❑ Replace all instances of *(trademark)* in the document with the trademark symbol (™). Ensure that you replace only instances in which the word *trademark* is in parentheses, and no other version of the word.

Tip Enter the trademark symbol in the document, cut it to the Clipboard, and then choose *Clipboard Contents* as the replacement.

➤ Save the **Word_2-1** document. Open the **Word_2-1_results** document and compare the two documents to check your work. Then close the open documents.

Objective 2.2: Format text and paragraphs

Format text

You can apply basic font formatting to text by using the tools available in the Font group on the Home tab and in the Font dialog box. (Some font settings are also available on the Mini Toolbar that appears when you select text.)

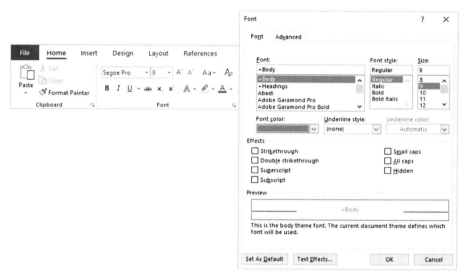

Tools for applying font formatting

Exam Strategy Exam MO-100 requires you to demonstrate that you can apply local font formatting to text. You must be able to change the font, size, color, style, and effects. Ensure that you know which font formatting settings are available only in the Font dialog box.

If you apply a series of formats to a selection of text—for example, if you format a word as 14-point, bold, italic, red text—and then want to apply the same combination of formatting to other text, you can quickly do so by using the Format Painter. When using the Format Painter, you first copy existing formatting from text characters, a paragraph, or an object, and then paste the formatting to other text or objects.

You can use the Format Painter to paste copied formatting only once or to remain active until you turn it off.

Use the Format Painter to copy all the formatting from one element to another

To open the Font dialog box

→ On the **Home** tab, in the **Font** group, click the dialog box launcher.

→ Right-click any document text, and then click **Font**.

→ Press **Ctrl+D**.

To copy existing formatting to other text

1. Select the text that has the formatting you want to copy.

2. On the **Mini Toolbar** or in the **Clipboard** group on the **Home** tab, click the **Format Painter** button once if you want to apply the copied formatting only once, or twice if you want to apply the copied formatting multiple times.

3. Click or select the text to which you want to apply the copied formatting.

4. If you clicked the **Format Painter** button twice, click or select additional text you want to format. Then click the **Format Painter** button again, or press the **Esc** key, to turn off the Format Painter.

Apply text effects

In older versions of Word, you could create specialized WordArt text objects that had set combinations of effects applied to them. In Word 2019, you can apply text effects directly to text, or if you want the flexibility of positioning the text anywhere on the page, you can create WordArt objects that have the same text effects applied.

These effects can include outlines, fills, shadows, reflections, glow effects, beveled edges, and three-dimensional rotation. You can modify the effects whether they are applied directly to text or to WordArt objects.

Exam Strategy Creating and modifying WordArt is not tested on the MOS exams for Word 2019.

If you want to simply apply text effects directly to text, you do so from the Text Effects And Typography menu that is available from the Font group on the Home tab. You can apply a preset combination or set each effect independently.

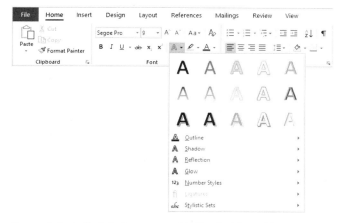

You apply text effects just as you would other font formatting

To apply preconfigured text effects to selected text

→ On the **Home** tab, in the **Font** group, click the **Text Effects and Typography** button, and then click the effect you want to apply.

Format paragraphs

You can change paragraph attributes such as alignment, indentation, spacing, shading, and borders from the Paragraph group on the Home tab, and from the Paragraph dialog box.

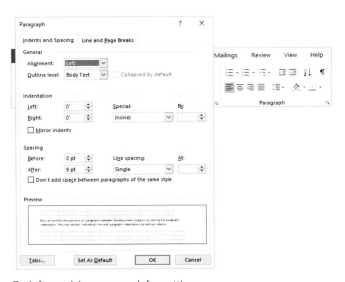

Tools for applying paragraph formatting

See Also For information about the Line And Page Breaks tab of the Paragraph dialog box, see "Objective 2.3: Create and configure document sections."

You can control the position of paragraphs between the document margins by setting the paragraph indentation. You can control individual line and paragraph indentation by setting indents from the left and right sides of the paragraph. You can set four types of indents:

- **First Line indent** The paragraph's first line of text begins at this setting.
- **Hanging indent** The paragraph's second and subsequent lines of text begin at this setting.
- **Left indent** The left side of the paragraph aligns with this setting.
- **Right indent** The paragraph text wraps when it reaches this setting.

When the rulers are displayed, markers on the horizontal ruler indicate the individual indent settings. You can modify the indent settings on the Layout tab, in the Paragraph dialog box, or by dragging the markers on the ruler.

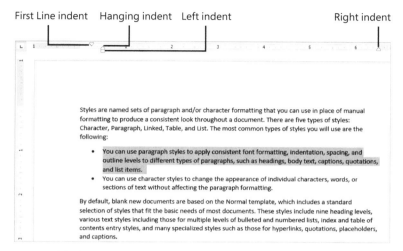

Paragraph indentation markers on the ruler

A paragraph has two vertical spacing measurements: *line spacing* (the space between the lines within the paragraph) and *paragraph spacing* (the space before and after the paragraph).

Line spacing and paragraph spacing are initially set by the style that is applied to the paragraph. You can modify the paragraph spacing by manually formatting the paragraph, modifying the style, changing the style set, or changing the paragraph spacing setting for the entire document.

To open the Paragraph dialog box

→ On the **Home** tab or **Layout** tab, click the **Paragraph** dialog box launcher.

→ On the **Home** tab, in the **Paragraph** group, click the **Line and Paragraph Spacing** button, and then click **Line Spacing Options**.

→ Right-click anywhere in a paragraph, and then click **Paragraph**.

To set the indentation of selected paragraphs

➜ Open the **Paragraph** dialog box, and display the **Indents and Spacing** tab. In the **Indentation** area, specify the **Left**, **Right**, and **Special** settings. Then click **OK**.

➜ On the **Home** tab, in the **Paragraph** group, click the **Increase Indent** or **Decrease Indent** button to change only the left indent.

➜ On the **Layout** tab, in the **Paragraph** group, in the **Indent** area, specify the **Left** or **Right** settings.

Tip To increase or decrease paragraph indentation beyond the margins, specify negative Left and Right settings.

➜ On the horizontal ruler, drag the **First Line Indent**, **Hanging Indent**, **Left Indent**, and **Right Indent** markers.

To set the spacing of selected paragraphs

➜ Open the **Paragraph** dialog box, and display the **Indents and Spacing** tab. In the **Spacing** area, specify the **Before**, **After**, and **Line spacing** settings. If you want to maintain the line spacing between paragraphs of the same style, select the **Don't add space between paragraphs of the same style** check box. Then click **OK**.

➜ On the **Layout** tab, in the **Paragraph** group, in the **Spacing** area, specify the **Before** or **After** setting.

➜ On the **Home** tab, in the **Paragraph** group, click the **Line and Paragraph Spacing** button, and then do either of the following:

• Click **Add Space Before Paragraph**, **Remove Space Before Paragraph**, **Add Space After Paragraph**, or **Remove Space After Paragraph** to change the external spacing. (Only two options will be visible, depending on the current settings of the active paragraph.)

• Click **1.0**, **1.15**, **1.5**, **2.0**, **2.5**, or **3.0** to select a standard line spacing.

To set paragraph spacing for an entire document

→ On the **Design** tab, in the **Document Formatting** group, click **Paragraph Spacing** and then click **Default**, **No Paragraph Space**, **Compact**, **Tight**, **Open**, **Relaxed**, or **Double**.

→ On the **Paragraph Spacing** menu, click **Custom Paragraph Spacing**. On the **Set Defaults** tab of the **Manage Styles** dialog box, in the **Paragraph Spacing** area, specify the **Before**, **After**, and **Line spacing** settings. Then click **OK**.

Exam Strategy You can quickly and consistently modify the spacing and indentation of all paragraphs of a specific style by modifying the style. Exam MO-100 requires that you demonstrate the manual application of paragraph formatting. Modifying and creating styles is part of the objective domain for Exam MO-101, "Microsoft Word Expert."

Apply built-in styles to text

Styles are named sets of paragraph and/or character formatting that you can use in place of manual formatting to produce a consistent look throughout a document. There are five types of styles: Character, Paragraph, Linked, Table, and List. The most common types of styles you will use are the following:

- **Paragraph styles** You can use these styles to apply consistent font formatting, indentation, spacing, and outline levels to different types of paragraphs, such as headings, body text, captions, quotations, and list items.

See Also Paragraph outline levels control the content of the Headings page of the Navigation pane and of tables of contents that you generate by using the Word feature. For information about the Navigation pane, see "Objective 1.1: Navigate within documents." For information about tables of contents, see "Objective 4.2: Create and manage reference tables."

- **Character styles** You can use these styles to change the appearance of individual characters, words, or sections of text without affecting the paragraph formatting.

By default, blank new documents are based on the Normal template, which includes a standard selection of styles that fit the basic needs of most documents. These styles include nine heading levels, various text styles including those for multiple levels of bulleted and numbered lists, index and table of contents entry styles, and many specialized styles such as those for hyperlinks, quotations, placeholders, and captions.

You can view the available styles in several locations, including the following:

- On the Home tab of the ribbon, the Styles gallery displays samples of selected styles. Part of the Styles gallery is always visible in the Styles group—the number of visible styles depends on the width of your program window and screen resolution. You can scroll the gallery pane or expand it to display all the styles at once.

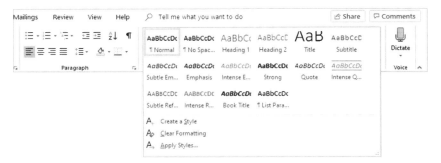

The Styles gallery displaying the recommended built-in styles

---

Tip Only styles that have been added to the Styles gallery appear in it; you can add, remove, and reorder the styles in the gallery to suit your needs.

- The Styles pane displays all the currently available styles or a subset thereof that you designate, such as only those that are currently in use. You can display or hide the Styles pane and configure it to display only style names (the default) or samples of the styles.

Tip On the right side of the Styles pane, paragraph marks indicate paragraph styles, the letter *a* identifies character styles, and a combination of the two identifies linked styles that can be applied to either paragraphs or characters. Pointing to any style displays a ScreenTip detailing the formatting included in the style.

Style area pane   Style pane

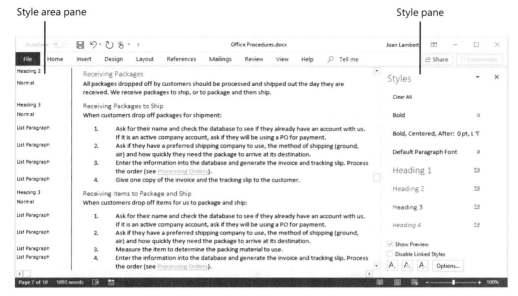

You can adjust the pane widths to maximize the content area

- At the left side of a document displayed in Draft view or Outline view, the *style area pane* displays the name of the style attached to each paragraph. (It does not display character styles.) You can turn on or off the display of the style area pane.

See Also For information about modifying the appearance of styles by changing style sets, see "Objective 1.2: Format documents."

To display the Styles pane in the program window

➔ On the **Home** tab, click the **Styles** dialog box launcher.

To display visual representations of styles in the Styles pane

➔ At the bottom of the **Styles** pane, select the **Show Preview** check box.

To display a specific category of styles in the Styles pane

1. At the bottom of the **Styles** pane, click **Options**.

2. In the **Style Pane Options** dialog box, do the following, and then click **OK**.

   - In the **Select styles to show** list, click **Recommended**, **In use**, **In current document**, or **All styles**.

- In the **Select how list is sorted** list, click **Alphabetical**, **As Recommended**, **Font**, **Based on**, or **By type**.

- Select the check boxes for the types of formatting you want to show as styles.

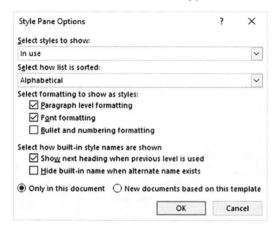

To display styles and style modifications, select the Paragraph Level Formatting and Font Formatting check boxes

To turn on or off the display of the style area pane in the Draft and Outline views

1. Open the **Word Options** dialog box, and display the **Advanced** page.

2. In the **Display** area, enter a positive number in the **Style area pane width in Draft and Outline views** box.

Word displays the style area pane only if its width is set to a measurement greater than zero

3. In the **Word Options** dialog box, click **OK**.

To display the style area pane in a document

1. Display the document in Draft view or Outline view.

2. If necessary, turn on the display of the style area pane.

To apply a character style

1. Select the text you want to format, or position the cursor anywhere in a single word you want to format.

2. In the **Styles** pane or **Styles** gallery, click the character style you want to apply.

To apply a paragraph style

1. Select or position the cursor anywhere in the paragraph you want to format.

2. In the **Styles** pane or **Styles** gallery, click the paragraph style you want to apply.

To modify the content of the Styles gallery

→ To add a style to the **Styles** gallery, right-click the style in the **Styles** pane, and then click **Add to Style Gallery**.

→ To remove a style from the **Styles** gallery, right-click the style in the **Styles** pane or **Styles** gallery, and then click **Remove from Style Gallery**.

Exam Strategy Exam MO-100 requires you to demonstrate the ability to apply existing styles. Modifying existing styles and creating new styles are part of the objective domain for Exam MO-101, "Microsoft Word 2019 Expert."

Clear formatting and styles

From time to time, you might want to remove manually applied formatting or styles from document content.

To remove manually applied formatting

→ Select the content that you want to revert to the settings of the applied styles, and then press **Ctrl+Spacebar**.

To clear styles

→ To revert selected content to the **Normal** style, do either of the following:

- In the **Styles** pane, click **Clear All**.

- On the **Home** tab, in the **Font** group, click the **Clear All Formatting** button.

→ To revert all content of a specific style to the **Normal** style, in the **Styles** pane, point to the style you want to clear, click the arrow that appears, and then click **Clear Formatting**. The command name indicates the number of instances of the selected style that are currently applied.

To remove highlighting from selected text

→ On the **Home** tab, in the **Font** group, click the **Text Highlight Color** arrow, and then click **No Color**.

Tip The standard methods for clearing formatting don't remove highlighting.

Exam Strategy The Microsoft Office Specialist exams must be completed within a specific amount of time. Learn and practice the techniques for performing tasks so that you can do so quickly.

Objective 2.2 practice tasks

The practice file for these tasks is in the **MOSWord2019\Objective2** practice file folder. The folder also contains a result file that you can use to check your work.

➤ Open the **Word_2-2** document, display the Navigation pane and the Styles pane.

➤ From the Styles pane, do the following:

❏ Display all the styles in the document, in alphabetical order.

❏ Select all paragraphs that are formatted as *Heading 3*.

❏ Apply the *Heading 2* style to the selected paragraphs. Note the document structure change in the Navigation pane.

➤ Move to the beginning of the document, and do the following:

❏ Apply the *Heading 1* style to the *Financial Summary* heading. Note the document structure change in the Navigation pane.

❏ Use the Format Painter to copy the style from the *Financial Summary* heading to the *Financial Statements* and *Statement Notes* headings.

❏ Set the paragraph spacing for the entire document to *Relaxed*.

➤ Immediately after the document title, select the text *A Brief Review of Our Finances*. Then do the following:

❏ Apply the *Fill: Green, Accent color 3; Sharp Bevel* text effect to the selected text.

❏ Center the paragraph horizontally on the page.

❏ Change the space before the Financial Summary heading from 20 pt to 12 pt.

➤ Save the **Word_2-2** document. Open the **Word_2-2_results** document and compare the two documents to check your work. Then close the open documents.

Objective 2.3: Create and configure document sections

The skills being tested by this objective are those related to controlling the layout of document content on pages by inserting custom page breaks, creating document sections that display content differently from the main document, and laying out the content of a document or section in columns.

You can format text in multiple columns, and manually divide a document into pages or sections. When you define sections, you can set up the pages of each section differently from other sections of the document.

By using sections, you can easily include multiple page configurations in one document

Display content in columns

By default, Word 2019 displays the content of a document in one column that spans the width of the page between the left and right margins. You can choose to display content in two or more columns to create layouts like those used in newspapers and magazines.

You can format an entire document or a section of a document in columns. When you select part of a document and format it in columns, Word inserts section breaks at the beginning and end of the selection to delineate the area in which the columnar formatting is applied. Content fills the first column on each page and then moves to the top of the next column. When all the columns on one page are full, the content moves to the next page. You can insert *column breaks* to specify where you want to end one column and start another. Section breaks and column breaks are visible when you display formatting marks in the document.

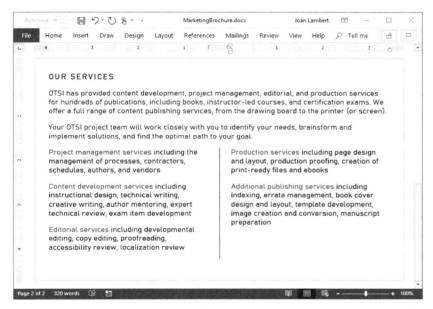

The ruler displays the column settings and the indent settings for the currently active column

When dividing text into columns, you can choose one, two, or three columns of equal width or two columns of unequal width. If the standard options don't suit your needs, you can specify the number and width of columns. The number of columns is limited by the width and margins of the page. Each column must be at least a half inch (or 1.27 centimeter) wide.

When you format selected content to display columns, Word automatically inserts section breaks before and after the selected content. (If you format an entire document in columns, no section breaks are inserted.)

To format selected text into simple columns

→ On the **Layout** tab, in the **Page Setup** group, click the **Columns** button, and then click the standard column configuration you want.

To manually break column content

→ Position the cursor where you want to insert the column break, and then do either of the following:

- On the **Layout** tab, in the **Page Setup** group, click the **Breaks** button, and then in the **Page Breaks** section, click **Column**.
- Press **Ctrl+Shift+Enter**.

To format all or part of a document in built-in column configurations

1. Do either of the following:

- To format all of the document content in columns, position the cursor anywhere in the document, but do not select content.
- To format part of the document content in columns, select the contiguous content.

2. On the **Layout** tab, in the **Page Setup** group, click the **Columns** button, and then do either of the following:

- To format the content in columns of equal width, click **Two** or **Three** (specifying the number of columns).
- To format the content into one narrow and one wide column, click **Left** or **Right** (specifying the location of the narrow column).

To format content in a preset column configuration

1. Select the contiguous content you want to format in columns, or to format the entire document, position the cursor in the document without selecting content.

2. On the **Layout** tab, in the **Page Setup** group, click the **Columns** button, and then click **More Columns**.

3. In the **Columns** dialog box, do the following, and then click **OK**:

- In the **Number of columns** box, enter or select the number of columns (up to 16) that you want to configure.
- Clear the **Equal column width** check box.

- In the **Width and spacing** area, set the width of each nonstandard column and the space between it and the next column. Word automatically updates the width and spacing of other columns to equal the total available space.

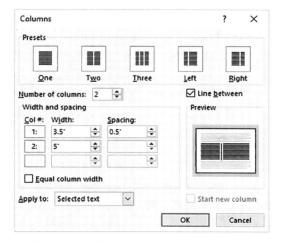

Configure content in up to 16 columns

To display lines between columns

→ In the **Columns** dialog box, select the **Line between** check box.

To insert a manual column break

→ Position the cursor to the left of the text that you want to start the next column, and then do either of the following:

- On the **Layout** tab, in the **Page Setup** group, click the **Breaks** button, and then click **Column**.
- Press **Ctrl+Shift+Enter**.

To revert content to a single column

→ Position the cursor in the columnar section, and then do any of the following:

- On the **Layout** tab, in the **Page Setup** group, click the **Columns** button, and then click **One**.
- Open the **Columns** dialog box. In the **Presets** area, click **One**. Then click **OK**.
- Delete the section break that defines the columnar section.

Define document pages and sections

When the content of a document exceeds the amount that will fit within the margins of a single page, Word creates a new page by inserting a *soft page break* (a page break that moves if the preceding content changes). If you want to break a page in a place other than where Word would normally break it, you can insert a manual page break. The content after the page break moves to the top of the next page.

Tip As you edit the content of a document, Word changes the location of the soft page breaks, but not of any manual page breaks that you insert.

If you want to control the page layout more specifically, you can insert a section break. Section breaks have two purposes:

- They can act as a "smart" page break and move the following content to the next page, the next even page, or the next odd page.
- They can fence off a portion of document content that you want to format differently from other content.

You divide a document into sections by inserting a section break at the beginning of each new section. (It is not necessary to have a section break at the beginning or end of a document.) You can choose from three types of section breaks:

- Continuous starts the new section on the same page.
- Next Page breaks the page before beginning the new section.
- Even Page begins the new section at the top of the next even-numbered page.
- Odd Page begins the new section at the top of the next odd-numbered page.

For each section, you can configure independent page setup options, including:

- Margins
- Pages to print per sheet
- Line numbers
- Orientation
- Headers and footers
- Borders
- Paper size
- Vertical alignment
- Shading

You can also format the content within a section into columns, as discussed in the previous topic of this section.

See Also For information about configuring page setup options for a document, see "Objective 1.2: Format documents."

A common use of section breaks is to set off content that you want to orient vertically on a page from content that you want to orient horizontally so that a single document can include both portrait and landscape pages.

Page and section breaks are visible in a document when paragraph and other formatting marks are shown. When working in a document that includes breaks, display the formatting marks for two reasons: so you don't accidentally move or delete page, column, or section breaks, and so you can locate the breaks if you want to move or delete them.

When displaying formatting marks, all types of manually placed breaks are shown. Page breaks are represented by dotted lines, section breaks by double-dotted lines, and column breaks by double-spaced dotted lines. Each type of break also has a text label.

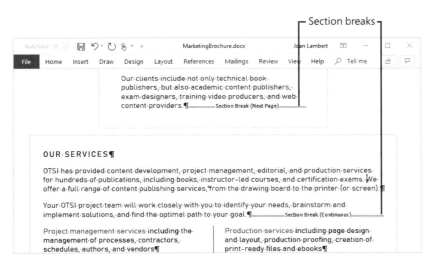

Breaks are shown with other formatting marks, as labeled, double-dotted lines

If you want a paragraph of text to start a new page regardless of other changes in the document content, you can configure the paragraph formatting to include a page break. When you use this method, the page break is not shown with the formatting marks.

To divide a document into sections

1. Position the cursor at the beginning of the content with which you want to start the new section.

2. On the **Layout** tab, in the **Page Setup** group, click the **Breaks** button.

3. On the **Breaks** menu, in the **Section Breaks** section, click **Next Page**, **Continuous**, **Even Page**, or **Odd Page** to define the starting page of the new section.

To insert a manual page break

1. Position the cursor to the left of the content that you want to start the new page.

2. Do any of the following:

    *   On the **Insert** tab, in the **Pages** group, click the **Page Break** button.
    *   On the **Layout** tab, in the **Page Setup** group, click the **Breaks** button, and then in the list, click **Page**.
    *   Press **Ctrl+Enter**.

To open the Paragraph dialog box

➜ On the **Home** tab, in the **Paragraph** group, click the dialog box launcher.

To force a page break before a specific paragraph

1. Position the cursor anywhere in the paragraph.

2. Open the **Paragraph** dialog box, and display the **Line and Page Breaks** tab.

3. In the **Pagination** area, select the **Page break before** check box. Then click **OK**.

You can configure a page break as part of the paragraph formatting

---

Tip If a page break should always appear before a specific type of paragraph, such as a heading, you can incorporate the Page Break Before setting into the paragraph's style.

To insert a section break

→ On the **Layout** tab, in the **Page Setup** group, click the **Breaks** button, and then in the **Section Breaks** section, click one of the following:

- To create a section that does not affect page breaks, click **Continuous**.

- To create a section that starts content on the next page, click **Next Page**.

- To create a section that starts content on the next even-numbered page, click **Even Page**.

- To create a section that starts content on the next odd-numbered page, click **Odd Page**.

To specify different settings for a document section

→ Position the cursor anywhere in the section you want to format, and then do either of the following:

- On the **Layout** tab, in the **Page Setup** group, change the **Margins**, **Orientation**, **Size**, **Columns**, **Line Numbers**, or **Hyphenation** setting. The change will apply to the current section only.

- Open the **Page Setup** dialog box. On the **Margins**, **Paper**, and **Layout** tabs, configure the settings that you want to change for the current section. In the **Apply to** list, click **This section**. Then click **OK**.

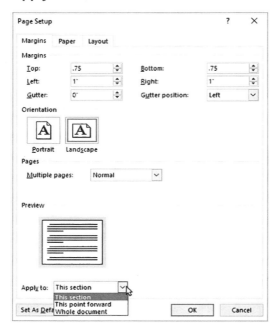

This Section appears in the Apply To list only when the document contains multiple sections

To display formatting marks (including page, section, and column breaks)

➜ On the **Home** tab, in the **Paragraph** group, click the **Show/Hide ¶** button.

➜ Press **Ctrl+Shift+8** (**Ctrl+***).

To remove a manual page break or section break

1. Display formatting marks.

2. Do any of the following:

   - Click in the left margin to select the page break or section break paragraph.

   - Drag to select the page break or section break marker.

   - Position the cursor to the left of the page break or section break marker.

3. Press **Delete**.

Objective 2.3 practice tasks

The practice file for these tasks is in the **MOSWord2019\Objective2** practice file folder. The folder also contains a result file that you can use to check your work.

➤ Open the **Word_2-3** document, and do the following:

☐ Near the beginning of the document, insert a page break before the *Process* heading.

☐ Select the *Questions for Team Leaders* and *Questions for Department Reps* headings and the lists that follow them. Format the selection in two columns of equal width. Set the space between the columns to **0.3"** and place a vertical line between the columns.

☐ If necessary, insert a column break before the *Questions for Department Reps* heading so that each list is in its own column.

☐ In the *Pre-Plan Project* section, select the heading, the paragraph, and the list items. Format each of the selected paragraphs to stay on the same page as the paragraph that follows it, and to keep all the lines of each paragraph together.

☐ Near the end of the document, locate the *Carry out project* section. Create a separate document section that contains only the content of the *Carry out project* section, on its own page. For only this section, set the orientation to *Landscape* and all four margins to **2"**.

☐ Preview the document on the Print page of the Backstage view to verify the changes.

➤ Save the **Word_2-3** document. Open the **Word_2-3_results** document and compare the two documents to check your work. Then close the open documents.

Objective group 3

Manage tables and lists

The skills tested in this section of the Microsoft Office Specialist exam for Microsoft Word 2019 relate to creating and modifying tables and lists. Specifically, the following objectives are associated with this set of skills:

- **3.1** Create tables
- **3.2** Modify tables
- **3.3** Create and modify lists

Some types of document content are easier to read when presented in a structured format—specifically, in a table or list. Tables are particularly useful for presenting numeric data, but also for organizing text. Numbered lists are an effective means of presenting information that has a specific order or for which you want to designate labels. Bulleted lists present unordered sets of information in a tidy format that is far more legible than running the information together in a long paragraph.

This chapter guides you in studying ways of creating, modifying, and formatting tables, bulleted lists, and numbered lists; and sorting table data.

> To complete the practice tasks in this chapter, you need the practice files contained in the **MOSWord2019\Objective3** practice file folder. For more information, see "Download the practice files" in this book's introduction.

Objective 3.1: Create tables

Data sets, particularly of numeric data, can often be presented more clearly and efficiently in a table than in a paragraph of text. Tables present large amounts of data, or complex data, in a format that is easier to read and understand by structuring it in rows and columns, which often include headers to explain the purpose or meaning of the data.

Tip When designing a table to meet accessibility standards, include row headers. For information about Word document accessibility, see "Objective 1.4: Inspect documents for issues."

You can create a table structure and then enter information in the table cells, you can convert existing text into a table, or you can copy and paste a table structure from another Microsoft Office file, such as an Excel worksheet, a PowerPoint slide, or an Access data table.

There are two simple methods for creating blank tables:

- The Insert Table menu displays a grid in which you select a range of cells—up to 10 columns wide and 8 rows high—to create a table of that size. When you create a table this way, each row is one line high and all the columns are of equal width.

- The Insert Table dialog box provides an interface in which you enter or select the number of rows and columns you want to create, and you can specify a fixed or relative column width.

Exam Strategy Exam MO-100 tracks the results you achieve, rather than the method you use to perform each task. In addition to the methods discussed in this topic, you can use the Draw Table feature to manually define table rows and columns on the document page; however, this isn't a very efficient method of creating a table, and you will not be required to demonstrate it on the exam.

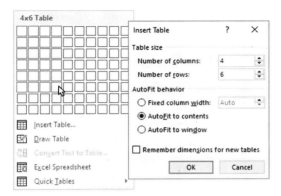

You can select AutoFit options when creating a table or any time thereafter

A table appears in the document as a set of cells, usually delineated by borders or gridlines. Each cell contains an end-of-cell marker, and each row ends with an end-of-row marker. These markers are visible only when hidden formatting marks are shown.

Tip Two separate elements in Word 2019 are named *gridlines*, and both can be used in association with tables. From the Show group on the View tab, you can display the *document gridlines* with which you can position content on the page. From the Table group on the Layout tool tab, you can display the *table gridlines* that define the cells of a table.

When you point to a table, a move handle appears in its upper-left corner and a size handle in its lower-right corner.

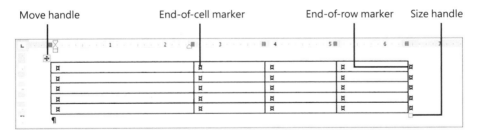

End-of-cell and end-of-row markers are visible only when formatting marks are displayed

---

Tip End-of-cell markers and end-of-row markers are identical in appearance. They are visible only when you display formatting marks in the document.

When the cursor is in a table, two Table Tools tabs—Design and Layout—appear on the ribbon.

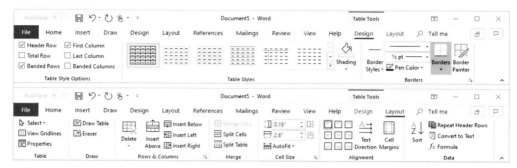

Table management tools are available from the contextual tabs and shortcut menu

Create tables from scratch or from text

Converting text to a table is particularly easy when the text has a consistent structure, such as that of a tabbed list. You can convert cell entries that are separated by tabs, commas, paragraph marks, or another single character. Similarly, you can convert any table to text that is separated by the same selection of characters.

Consistent text separation is key when converting between text and tables

When converting a table to text, the text separator that you choose affects the text layout.

Original table	
A1	B1
A2	B2

Converted to text

Paragraph mark separators	A1	
	B1	
	A2	
	B2	
Tab separators	A1	B1
	A2	B2
Comma separators	A1, B1	
	A2, B2	
Hyphen separators	A1-B1	
	A2-B2	

The effects of the standard text separator options

3

To create a blank page-width table with columns of equal width

1. On the **Insert** tab, in the **Tables** group, click the **Table** button.

2. In the grid, move the pointer across and down to select the number of columns and rows you want, and then click the lower-right cell in the selection.

To create a table and specify column fitting options

1. On the **Insert** tab, in the **Tables** group, click the **Table** button, and then click **Insert Table**.

2. In the **Insert Table** dialog box, in the **Table size** area, specify the number of columns and rows you want the table to include.

3. In the **AutoFit behavior** area, do one of the following, and then click **OK**:

   - To specify the width of the table columns, click **Fixed column width**, and then enter the width in the box.

   - To size the table columns to fit their contents, click **AutoFit to contents**. The width of the resulting table may be less than the width of the page.

   - To create a page-width table that is divided into columns of equal width, click **AutoFit to window**.

> **See Also** After creating a table, it is common to change the size of one or more columns to fit your needs. For information about resizing columns, see "Objective 3.2: Modify tables."

To convert text to a table

1. Ensure that the text you want to convert uses a consistent method of separating the content that will go into the table cells.

2. Select the text that you want to convert.

3. On the **Insert** tab, in the **Tables** group, click the **Table** button, and then click **Convert Text to Table**.

4. In the **Convert Text to Table** dialog box, in the **Separate text at** section, click or enter the cell text separator. Word evaluates the selected text and indicates the number of rows and columns that will fit it.

5. In the **Table size** section, review the **Number of columns** entry against the selected content and adjust it as necessary.

   > **Tip** If the Number Of Columns or Number Of Rows setting doesn't seem correct, the selected text might not use consistent text separators.

6. Adjust the **Table size** and **AutoFit behavior** settings, select the type of text separator, and then click **OK**.

To convert a table to text

1. Select or click anywhere in the table.

2. On the **Layout** tool tab, in the **Data** group, click **Convert to Text**.

3. In the **Convert Table To Text** dialog box, click the text separator you want to use, and then click **OK**:

   - To put each cell entry in its own paragraph, click **Paragraph marks**.

   - To put the cell entries from each row into one paragraph, do any of the following:

     - To create a tabbed list with the same number of columns as the table, click **Tabs**.

     - To put a comma and space between cell entries, click **Commas**.

     - To put any single character between cell entries, click **Other** and enter the character in the **Other** box.

Apply table styles

To quickly and professionally format a table, you can apply one of the built-in table styles. These include a variety of borders, shading choices, text colors, and other attributes to give the table a professional look. When formatting a table, you can choose the table elements that you want to emphasize, such as a header or total row or the first or last column, and you can format the table with banded columns or rows to make the contents more legible.

Tip When table cells aren't defined by borders or other formatting, you can display nonprinting gridlines to more easily identify individual cells.

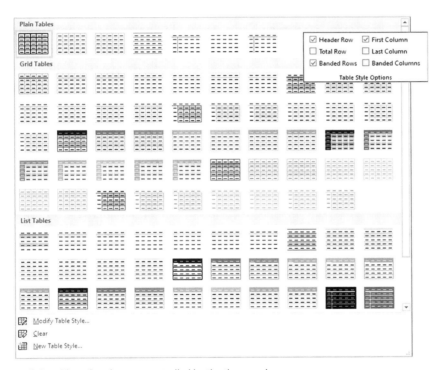

Built-in table style colors are controlled by the theme colors

To apply a built-in table style

1. Click anywhere in the table you want to format.

2. On the **Design** tool tab, in the **Table Styles** gallery, click the built-in style you want to apply.

To emphasize table elements

→ On the **Design** tool tab, in the **Table Style Options** group, select the check boxes of the table elements you want to emphasize.

To manually format table elements

→ To shade cells, columns, or rows, select the element and then on the **Design** tool tab, in the **Table Styles** group, click the **Shading** arrow and select the color you want.

→ To change the color or width of borders, on the **Design** tool tab, in the **Borders** group, select the border style, line style, line weight, and pen color you want, and then do either of the following:

- On the **Borders** menu, click the border configuration that you want to insert with the selected settings.

- Click the **Border Painter** button, and then click individual table borders to apply the selected settings.

→ To remove selected cell borders, do either of the following:

- Select one or more cells, rows, or columns from which you want to remove the borders. Then on the **Design** tool tab, in the **Borders** group, on the **Borders** menu, click **No Border**.

- On the **Layout** tool tab, in the **Draw** group, click the **Eraser** button, and then click individual table borders to remove them. Click the **Eraser** button again, press **Esc**, or click away from the table to turn off the feature.

To display or hide table gridlines

→ On the **Layout** tool tab, in the **Table** group, click the **View Gridlines** button.

To format text in tables

→ Select the text and format it as you would regular text, by clicking buttons on the **Mini Toolbar** and in the **Font**, **Paragraph**, and **Quick Styles** groups on the **Home** tab.

Objective 3.1 practice tasks

The practice file for these tasks is in the **MOSWord2019\Objective3** practice file folder. The folder also contains a result file that you can use to check your work.

➤ Open the **Word_3-1** document.

➤ In the *Consultation Request* section, convert the five paragraphs that follow the heading into a page-width table with five equal-width columns.

➤ In the *Mileage* section, do the following:

  ❑ Convert the tabbed list into a table that has two columns and six rows. Ensure that each column exactly fits its contents.

  ❑ Apply the *Grid Table 4 – Accent 1* built-in table style to the table. Configure the table style options to emphasize the header row and to have banded columns. (Clear all other check boxes.)

➤ In the *Consultation* section, convert the table to a tabbed list.

➤ In the *Estimate* section, do the following:

  ❑ In the blank paragraph below the heading, insert an empty table that is three columns wide and four rows high.

  ❑ Set each column to a width of exactly 1.5".

  ❑ Apply the *List Table 5 Dark – Accent 1* built-in table style to the table, with the default table style options.

➤ Save the **Word_3-1** document. Open the **Word_3-1_results** document. Check your work by comparing the open documents. Then close the open documents.

Objective 3.2: Modify tables

Sort table data

You can sort the data within a table by the contents of one or more table columns. Word sorts only the data rows in your table, and not the header row or Total row (if your table includes either of these options).

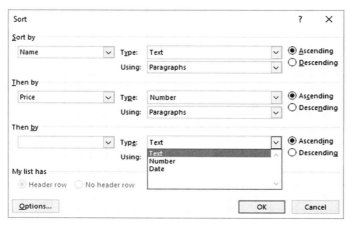

You can sort the data in a table by multiple columns

To activate a table for editing

➜ Select or click anywhere in the table.

To sort table data

1. Activate the table for editing.

2. On the **Layout** tool tab, in the **Data** group, click the **Sort** button. The Sort dialog box opens, with the table's column headers available in the Sort By and Then By lists. If headers aren't configured in the table style options, the list entries are (Column 1), (Column 2), and so on.

3. If your table includes headers and the Sort function didn't identify them as such, click **Header row** in the **My list has** section near the bottom of the dialog box to add the headers to the Sort By and Then By lists.

4. In the **Sort by** section, select the primary column by which you want to sort the content. Verify that the **Sort** function has correctly identified the **Type** and **Using** settings, and then click **Ascending** or **Descending** to specify the sort order.

5. If you want to perform a nested sort on additional criteria, repeat step 4 in one or both of the **Then by** sections.

6. In the **Sort** dialog box, click **OK**.

◇◇

Exam Strategy Create a table that contains multiple columns and many rows of data and observe the effect of sorting the table by various columns, with and without a header row, to understand the sorting process.

◇◇

Modify table structure

You can modify a table's structure at any time. The basic ways to do so are as follows:

- Insert or delete rows or columns.

- Change the height or width of the table, columns, or rows.

- Modify the alignment and spacing within cells.

- Merge multiple cells into one cell or split one cell into multiple cells.

Merged cells   Wrapped text   Insert Column control

Floor	Room	Item	Action	Quantity	Cost ($)
	Kitchen	Refrigerator gasket	Replace	2	80
	Kitchen	Refrigerator water filter	Replace	1	30
1	Kitchen	Pendant lights	Replace	3	150
	Kitchen	Range hood controls	Repair	1	25
	Kitchen	Oven	Repair	1	150
	Kitchen	Dishwasher hinge	Repair	1	60
	Kitchen	Dishwasher rinse aid cap	Replace	1	12
	Bedroom #2	Carpet (stains & bleach)	Repair	1	50
2	BR#2 bathroom	Shower rail	Replace	1	45
	Hall bathroom	Shower rail	Replace	1	45
	Master bedroom	Closet ceiling	Repair	1	25
	Media room	Carpet (stains)	Repair	1	25

Inserting a column within an existing table structure

This topic reviews methods you can use to accomplish these tasks.

Tip You can move a table by pointing to it and then dragging the move handle that appears in the table's upper-left corner. Or you can click the move handle to select the table, and then use the Cut and Paste commands.

Insert and delete rows and columns

As you develop your table content, you might need to add or remove rows or columns.

To insert a row or column

→ Point to the left edge of the table, between two rows where you want to insert another, or to the top of the table between two columns where you want to insert another. A gray insertion indicator labeled with a plus sign appears as you approach a possible insertion point (after any existing row or column). When the plus sign turns blue, click to insert the row or column where indicated.

→ To insert a row at the end of a table, click in the last cell of the last row, and then press **Tab** to create a new row with the same formatting as the previous row.

Or

1. Position the cursor in a cell adjacent to which you want to insert a row or column.

2. On the **Layout** tool tab, in the **Rows & Columns** group, do either of the following:

    • To insert a row, click **Insert Above** or **Insert Below**.

    • To insert a column, click **Insert Left** or **Insert Right**.

Exam Strategy The Insert commands are available on the Mini Toolbar that appears when you select table content; however, that feature might be unavailable in the exam environment.

To insert multiple rows or columns

1. Select the number of existing rows or columns that you want to insert in the table, adjacent to the location you want to insert them.

2. On the **Layout** tool tab, in the **Rows & Columns** group, do either of the following:

    • To insert the selected number of rows, click **Insert Above** or **Insert Below**.

    • To insert the selected number of columns, click **Insert Left** or **Insert Right**.

To delete a table, rows, or columns

1. Click anywhere in the table, row, or column you want to delete, or select the rows or columns you want to delete.

2. On the **Layout** tool tab, in the **Rows & Columns** group, on the **Delete** menu, click **Delete Rows**, **Delete Columns**, or **Delete Table**.

Configure cell alignment and spacing

You can specify the alignment of content within table cells not only horizontally—Left, Center, and Right—but also vertically—Top, Center, and Bottom. There are nine alignment combinations in all, available from the Layout tool tab. They are visually identified in the Alignment group on the Layout tool tab.

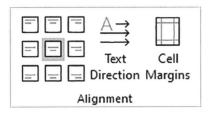

The alignment buttons are arranged and labeled to be easily identifiable

Tip Many programs refer to the vertical alignment positions as Top, Middle, and Bottom. Word 2019 labels both the horizontal and vertical center-alignment positions as Center.

Each cell within a table has internal margins that define the amount of space within the cell that content can occupy. By default, cells have only left and right margins. You can also specify top and bottom margins if you want to ensure that content has a minimum amount of padding for readability.

Cell margins and cell spacing affect the entire table

Tip Cell margins affect the space available within the cell for content. Cell spacing makes the surrounding cells smaller.

To configure internal and external table cell spacing

1. Activate the table.

2. On the **Layout** tool tab, in the **Alignment** group, click the **Cell Margins** button to open the Table Options dialog box.

3. In the **Table Options** dialog box, do any of the following, and then click **OK**.

    -   In the **Default cell margins** section, enter or select the amount of space you want Word to leave clear of content inside of each cell.

    -   In the **Default cell spacing** section, if you want to insert blank space between cells, select the **Allow spacing between cells** check box and then enter the cell spacing in the box.

    -   In the **Options** section, if you want to prevent the cell size from changing with the content, clear the **Automatically resize to fit contents** check box.

Merge and split cells

There are many circumstances in which you might want to merge the contents of two cells, either horizontally or vertically, or split one cell into multiple cells. Each of these operations changes the table from a simple grid to a more complex structure.

To create cells that span multiple rows or columns

→ Select the adjacent cells you want to connect. Then on the **Layout** tool tab, in the **Merge** group, click the **Merge Cells** button.

To divide a selected cell into multiple cells

1. On the **Layout** tool tab, in the **Merge** group, click the **Split Cells** button.

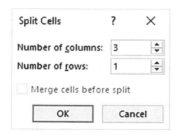

One cell can be split into up to 63 columns and 30 rows

2. In the **Split Cells** dialog box, specify the number of columns and rows into which you want to divide the cell, and then click **OK**.

IMPORTANT Some operations (adding or removing columns or rows) aren't possible when part of a table has merged cells. If you need to modify a table and the operation you want to perform is restricted, revert the split or merged cells to their original form, perform the operation, and then repeat the split or merge process.

Resize tables, rows, and columns

Some tables are the width of the page and others are narrower to fit their contents without leaving a lot of white space. You can change the dimensions of a table by changing the width of the columns or the height of the rows; you can also change the dimensions of the columns and rows by changing the width of the table.

Table, row, and column size can be set in the document, on the ruler, or in the Table Properties dialog box. When working in the document, use the controls located in the Cell Size group on the Layout tool tab.

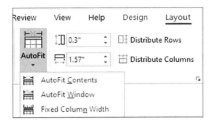

Some of the many tools for adjusting the row height and column width

When you display the ruler and activate a table, markers on the ruler indicate the table column and row dividers and the margin indents of the active column.

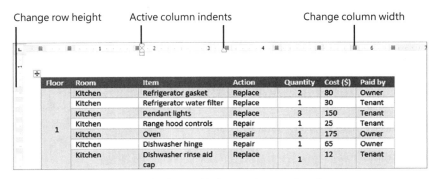

Activate any cell to display its dividers and indent markers on the rulers

See Also For information about the different types of indent markers, see "Objective 2.2: Format text and paragraphs."

To open the Table Properties dialog box

➜ Right-click anywhere in the table, and then click **Table Properties**.

Or

1. Click anywhere in the table or select any table element.

2. On the **Layout** tool tab, in the **Table** group, click the **Properties** button.

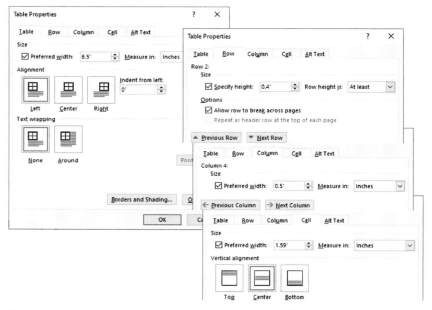

Table and column width can be set by percentage of the available space or in inches

To modify table structure from the Table Properties dialog box

➜ On the **Table** tab, set the table width in inches or percentage of the page width.

➜ On the **Row** tab, set the height of the selected rows.

➜ On the **Column** tab, set the preferred width of the selected column or columns.

➜ On the **Cell** tab, set the width of selected cells.

To select table elements

➜ Click anywhere in the table, column, row, or cell you want to select. On the **Layout** tool tab, in the **Table** group, on the **Select** menu, click **Select Cell**, **Select Column**, **Select Row**, or **Select Table**.

→ To select a table, point to the table, and then click the move handle that appears outside its upper-left corner.

→ To select a row, point to the left border of the row. When the pointer changes to a white, right-pointing arrow, click once.

→ To select a column, point to the top border of the column. When the pointer changes to a black, down-pointing arrow, click once.

→ To select a cell, triple-click the cell or click its left border.

→ To select adjacent rows, columns, or cells, do either of the following:

- Select the first row, column, or cell, hold down the **Shift** key, and then press the arrow keys.

- Drag across the rows, columns, or cells that you want to select.

→ To select non-adjacent rows, columns, or cells, select the first, hold down the **Ctrl** key, and then select the others.

To change the size of a selected table

→ Drag the size handle in the lower-right corner of the table. If you want to maintain the original aspect ratio of the table, hold down the **Shift** key while dragging the size handle.

→ On the **Table** tab of the **Table Properties** dialog box, specify the table width in inches or percentage of the available page width, and then click **OK**.

> **Tip** This book specifies measurements in inches. You can alternatively use your regional unit of measurement.

To change the height of a selected row

→ Drag the row's bottom border up or down.

→ Drag the row's **Adjust Table Row** marker on the vertical ruler up or down.

→ On the **Layout** tool tab, in the **Cell Size** group, change the **Table Row Height** setting.

→ On the **Row** tab of the **Table Properties** dialog box, specify the exact or minimum row height, and then click **OK**.

> **Tip** Setting a minimum row height enables the row height to increase when the height of cell content exceeds that measurement. You can set the row height in units such as pixels (px), but Word converts the measurement to inches when you save the changes.

→ With multiple rows selected, click the **Distribute Rows** button in the **Cell Size** group on the **Layout** tool tab, or right-click the selection and then click **Distribute Rows Evenly**.

To change the width of a selected column

→ Double-click the column's right border to set it to the narrowest width that fits its content.

→ Drag the column's right border to the left or right.

→ Drag the column's **Move Table Column** marker on the horizontal ruler to the left or right.

→ On the **Layout** tool tab, in the **Cell Size** group, change the **Table Column Width** setting.

→ On the **Column** tab of the **Table Properties** dialog box, specify the column width in inches or percentage of the table width, and then click **OK**.

To change the width of multiple columns

→ To equalize the width of contiguous columns, select the columns, and then do either of the following:

• On the **Layout** tool tab, in the **Cell Size** group, click the **Distribute Columns** button.

• Right-click the selection, and then click **Distribute Columns Evenly**.

→ To relatively size all columns into a page-width table, activate the table, and then on the **Layout** tool tab, in the **Cell Size** group, click **AutoFit** and then **AutoFit Window**.

→ To fit all columns in a table to their contents, select or click anywhere in the table, and then on the **Layout** tool tab, in the **Cell Size** group, click **AutoFit** and then **AutoFit Contents**.

Manage long tables

A table can run across multiple pages. When it does (or if it might), you can configure the table to display a copy of the header row at the top of each subsequent page. You can't select or modify the dynamic header row; any changes must be made in the actual table header. Repeating the header row helps readers of a document to more easily interpret data in multipage tables. It also allows assistive devices such as screen readers to correctly interpret the table contents.

In some cases, you might find that you want to manually split a large table into two or more tables, perhaps to move part of the data to another location in the document.

To repeat the table header row on subsequent pages

1. Position the cursor in the table header row.

2. Do either of the following:

   - On the **Layout** tool tab, in the **Data** group, click the **Repeat Header Rows** button.

   - Open the **Table Properties** dialog box, display the **Row** tab, select the **Repeat as header row at the top of each page** check box, and then click **OK**.

   IMPORTANT The Repeat Header Rows button and Repeat As Header Row option are active only when the cursor is in the header row.

To split a table

1. Position the cursor anywhere in the row that you want to be the first row of the new table that Word creates when you split the original table.

2. On the **Layout** tool tab, in the **Merge** group, click the **Split Table** button.

   The active row becomes the header row of the new table.

   Tip If you intend to split the table in more places, do so before resetting the header so you can save time by copying the header only once and then pasting it to the new tables.

To duplicate the original table header after splitting a table

1. Select and copy the original table header.

2. Position the cursor in the first cell of the new table, and then paste the copied header row.

Objective 3.2 practice tasks

The practice file for these tasks is in the **MOSWord2019\Objective3** practice file folder. The folder also contains a result file that you can use to check your work.

➤ Open the **Word_3-2** document, and do the following:

☐ In the *Customer List* section, delete the *ID* column from the table.

☐ Perform a nested sort to sort the table in ascending order by *State*, then by *City*, and then by *LastName*. Review the results.

☐ Delete all rows that contain contacts located in *Boston, MA*.

☐ Add two blank columns to the right side of the table. In the header row, enter **Date** at the top of the first blank column and **Time** at the top of the second blank column.

☐ Add a blank row to the top of the table. Notice that it becomes the header row.

☐ In the header row, merge the cells above the *Last Name*, *First Name*, *Address*, *City*, and *State* columns into one cell. Enter **Customer** in the merged cell. Then merge the cells above the *Date* and *Time* columns and enter **Appointment** in the merged cell.

☐ Select the second row of the table and format the text as bold.

☐ Center the text of the top two rows horizontally and vertically within the cells.

☐ Change the width of the table to **100 Percent** of the page width.

☐ Select the table rows that contain customer information. Set the height of the rows to **0.4"** and the cell alignment to *Align Center Left*.

☐ Scroll to page 2 of the document, which now contains several rows of the table. Configure the table to repeat the *Customer/Appointment* header row at the top of the second page.

➤ Save the **Word_3-2** document. Open the **Word_3-2_results** document. Check your work by comparing the open documents. Then close the documents.

Objective 3.3: Create and modify lists

Lists are paragraphs that start with a character and are formatted with a hanging indent so that the characters stand out on the left end of each list item. You can format an existing set of paragraphs as a bulleted, numbered, or multilevel list, or create the list as you enter information into the document. You can choose list starting characters from a library of preselected bullet symbols and numbering patterns, or you can create your own.

1. In this document, *Office 365* refers to new resources and *Contoso* refers to old resources. The Contoso resources will remain available for 30 days and then will be phased out.
2. Your Office 365 credentials are:
   - User name = first.last@wingtiptoys.com
   - Password = Your employee number

   You will be prompted to change your password the first time you sign in to the SharePoint site.
3. Contractors will continue to sign in to the SharePoint site by using their existing credentials; there is no change for non-employees at this time.
4. To add your Office 365 email account to Outlook:
   a. In the Account Settings window, select New.
   b. Provide your name, email address, and Office 365 password, and then select Next. The auto-configuration utility will connect to your Office 365 account.
   c. When the wizard finishes, close it and restart Outlook.

A list can contain a mix of numbered and bulleted items

After you create a bulleted or numbered list, you can modify the content and formatting of the list items, or even change the list type. You can change the bullet symbols, numeric characters, and list item levels. When working with numbered lists, you can manage the numbering so that the values start or restart as necessary.

Tip List levels are similar to outline levels—a standard list is Level 1, a sublist of a list item is Level 2, a sublist of a sublist item is Level 3, and so on. The built-in list formats support nine list levels.

Exam Strategy To pass Exam MO-100 and become certified as a Microsoft Office Specialist Associate in Word 2019, you must demonstrate that you can create bulleted and numbered lists, change the level of selected list items, manage the starting values of numbered lists, change bullet characters and define custom bullets, and change number formats and define custom number formats.

Create and manage bulleted lists

To create a bulleted list

1. Enter the list items as separate paragraphs, and then select the paragraphs.

2. On the **Home** tab, in the **Paragraph** group, do either of the following:

   - To use the standard bullet, click the **Bullets** button.

   - To select a bullet, click the **Bullets** arrow and then, in the **Bullet Library**, click the bullet symbol you want to display before each list item.

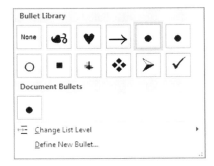

The symbols in your Bullet Library include default symbols and those you've recently used in lists

Or

1. Enter * (an asterisk) at the beginning of a paragraph, press the **Spacebar** or the **Tab** key, enter the first list item, and then press **Enter**.

2. Enter items and press **Enter** to add subsequent bulleted items.

3. To end the list, do one of the following:

   - To start the next paragraph at the left margin, press **Enter** twice.

   - To indent the next paragraph at the same level as the list, press **Enter** and then press **Backspace** or click **None** in the Bullet Library.

Tip If you want to start a paragraph with an asterisk or number but don't want to format the paragraph as a bulleted or numbered list, click the AutoCorrect Options button that appears after Word changes the formatting, and then in the list, click the appropriate Undo option. You can also click the Undo button on the Quick Access Toolbar.

To change the bullet symbol of bulleted list items

1. Select the list items you want to change the symbol for, or, to change all items in a list, click anywhere in the list.

2. On the **Home** tab, in the **Paragraph** group, click the **Bullets** arrow, and then in the **Bullet Library**, click the symbol you want to use.

To define custom bullets

1. On the **Home** tab, in the **Paragraph** group, click the **Bullets** arrow, and then click **Define New Bullet**.

2. In the **Define New Bullet** dialog box, do one of the following, and then click **OK** to add the bullet to the Bullet Library.

   - Click the **Symbol** button. In the **Symbol** dialog box, locate and click the bullet symbol you want to use, and then click **OK**.

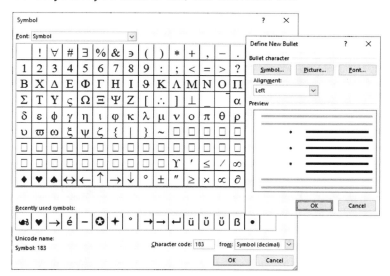

Choose a symbol from the Symbol font or choose a different font in the Font list

   - Click the **Picture** button. In the **Insert Pictures** dialog box, locate and click the bullet graphic you want to use, and then click **OK**.

   - To override the document font, click the **Font** button, select the font attributes you want in the **Font** dialog box, and then click **OK**.

   - In the **Alignment** list, click **Left**, **Centered**, or **Right** to specify the bullet alignment.

Create and manage numbered lists

To create a numbered list

→ Select the paragraphs you want to include in the list. On the **Home** tab, in the **Paragraph** group, do one of the following:

- Click the **Numbering** button to apply the standard numbered list format.

- Click the **Numbering** arrow and then click the numbering format you want the list to follow.

The standard number formats include a mix of numbers and roman numerals

Or

1. Enter **1.** (the number 1 followed by a period) at the beginning of a paragraph, press the **Spacebar** or the **Tab** key, enter the first list item, and then press **Enter**.

2. Enter items and press **Enter** to add subsequent numbered items.

3. To end the list, do one of the following:

- To start the next paragraph at the left margin, press **Enter** twice.

- To indent the next paragraph at the same level as the list, press **Enter** and then press **Backspace** or click **None** in the Numbering Library.

Tip The following procedure applies both to bulleted lists and to numbered lists.

To change the level of an active list item

→ Select the list item or items you want to change, and then do any of the following:

- Press **Tab** to demote the items or **Shift+Tab** to promote the items.

- On the **Home** tab, in the **Paragraph** group, click the **Increase Indent** button to demote the items or the **Decrease Indent** button to promote the items.

- On the **Home** tab, in the **Paragraph** group, click the **Bullets** arrow or the **Numbers** arrow, click **Change List Level**, and then in the **Change List Level** gallery, click the level you want.

To change the number format of numbered list items

1. Select the list items you want to format, or, to format all items in a list, click anywhere in the list.

2. On the **Home** tab, in the **Paragraph** group, click the **Numbering** arrow, and then click the number pattern you want to use.

3

To define a custom number format

1. On the **Home** tab, in the **Paragraph** group, click the **Numbering** arrow, and then click **Define New Number Format**.

2. In the **Define New Number Format** dialog box, do any of the following, and then click **OK** to add the number format to the **Numbering Library** area of the **Numbering** menu:

   - In the **Number style** list, click the numbering style you want to use.

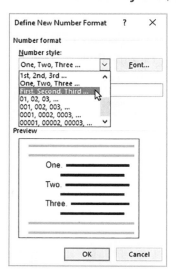

Specify the numbering style and any unchanging characters you want to display before or after the number

   - If you want to override the document font, click the **Font** button, select the font attributes you want in the **Font** dialog box, and then click **OK**.

   - In the **Number format** box, enter any characters (such as a period or the word *Level*) that you want to insert before or after the number.

   - In the **Alignment** list, click **Left**, **Centered**, or **Right** to specify the number alignment.

To restart the numbering of a numbered list

→ Right-click the number of the first list item you want to change, and then click **Restart at 1**.

Or

1. Position the cursor in the list item from which you want to restart. (Subsequent list items will renumber to follow the value you set.)

2. On the **Numbering** menu, click **Set Numbering Value**.

3. In the **Set Numbering Value** dialog box, click **Start new list**, and then click **OK**.

To continue the numbering of a numbered list

→ Right-click the number of the first list item you want to change, and then click **Continue Numbering**.

Or

1. Position the cursor in the first list item you want to change.

2. On the **Numbering** menu, click **Set Numbering Value**.

3. In the **Set Numbering Value** dialog box, click **Continue from previous list**.

4. If you want to skip over numbered lists that are between the original list and the continuation, select the **Advance value** check box and then, in the **Set value to** box, enter the number you want to assign to the list item.

5. In the **Set Numbering Value** dialog box, click **OK**.

To set the starting value for all or part of a numbered list

1. Right-click the number of the first list item you want to change, and then click **Set Numbering Value**.

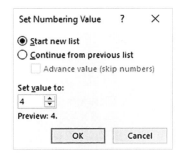

You can specify a list item number at the beginning of or within a list; the following items continue from the custom value

2. In the **Set Numbering Value** dialog box, in the **Set value to** box, enter or select the number you want to assign to the list item. Then click **OK**.

Objective 3.3 practice tasks

The practice file for these tasks is in the **MOSWord2019\Objective3** practice file folder. The folder also contains a result file that you can use to check your work.

➤ In the **Word 3-3** document, do the following:

❑ In the *Characters of a Hit Fantasy* section, format the four paragraphs as a bulleted list that uses the standard bullet character (•).

❑ In the sections titled *The Hero* and *The Teacher*, format the paragraphs as bulleted lists that use a custom bullet symbol of your choice from the Wingdings font.

❑ In the *Plot Elements of a Hit Fantasy* section, format the three paragraphs as a bulleted list that uses the four-diamond character (❖).

➤ In the section titled *The Sequence of Events*, do the following:

❑ Format the four paragraphs below the heading as a numbered list that uses the *A. B. C.* number format.

❑ Paste a copy of the list into the last blank paragraph of the document, and restart the list numbering. Change the number format of the second list to the *1) 2) 3)* format.

❑ Immediately below the second list, paste another copy of the list, and change it to a second-level list.

❑ Change the second-level list to a bulleted list that uses the square bullet character (▪).

➤ Save the **Word_3-3** document. Open the **Word_3-3_results** document. Check your work by comparing the open documents. Then close the open documents.

Objective group 4

Create and manage references

The skills tested in this section of the Microsoft Office Specialist exam for Microsoft Word 2019 relate to creating references within document content. Specifically, the following objectives are associated with this set of skills:

4.1   Create and manage reference elements

4.2   Create and manage reference tables

Word 2019 provides many ways of adding supporting information to a document for the purpose of referencing sources or aiding a reader in locating information, including these:

- To provide ancillary information without distracting the reader from the primary document content, you can insert links to footnotes at the bottom of the page or endnotes at the end of the document.

- To help readers locate specific information in the document, you can create a table of contents based on headings; a table of figures based on figure and table captions; and an index based on index entries.

- To provide information sources, you can create a bibliography based on content source citations and a table of authorities based on legal citations.

This chapter guides you in studying ways of creating footnotes, endnotes, bibliographical citations, bibliographies, and tables of contents.

> To complete the practice tasks in this chapter, you need the practice files contained in the **MOSWord2019\Objective4** practice file folder. For more information, see "Download the practice files" in this book's introduction.

◇◇

Exam Strategy To pass Exam MO-100 and become certified as a Microsoft Office Specialist Associate in Word 2019, you must demonstrate that you can create and manage tables of contents, footnotes and endnotes, bibliographical source citations, and bibliographies. Other reference-related tasks are part of the objective domain for Exam MO-101, "Microsoft Word Expert."

◇◇

Objective 4.1: Create and manage reference elements

Create and manage footnotes and endnotes

When you insert a footnote or endnote in the text of a document, a reference number, letter, or symbol appears at the insertion location. Your associated note, indicated by the same reference marker, appears in the location that you specify:

- You can place footnotes at the bottom of the page (relative to the margin) or immediately after the page content. The default location is at the bottom of the page, which provides a consistent experience for readers.

- You can place endnotes at the end of the document or, if a document contains multiple sections, at the end of the section. The default location is at the end of the document.

- In columnar text, you can place footnotes in one or multiple columns.

Two features help the reader to differentiate between the primary document content and the ancillary notes:

- In most views, a note separator line precedes footnote or endnote content.

- The default font size of footnote and endnote text is smaller than that of normal document text.

The front office space consists of a counter with three stations, each with phones and computer terminals with high-speed connections. The lobby provides a package preparation area and bins of retail items* for customers, and a bank of mailboxes. Empty the waste receptacles in the package preparation area every night or more often as needed to ensure a neat appearance. Check and restock the retail bins throughout the day as needed.†

The office hours are from 8:00 A.M. to 9:00 P.M., Monday through Saturday. Customers who rent mailboxes have access to them 24 hours a day.

---

* The loading dock staff will check items against the packing slip and then bring the slip to the office. The office employees are responsible for entering the packing slip information into the inventory database.
† Provided retail items include envelopes, tape, and marking pens.
‡ Office employees are responsible for both activities.

Footnotes are stacked from the bottom margin of the page upward

A document can contain both footnotes and endnotes. The decision to position a note as a footnote or as an endnote might be governed by your organization's editorial standards, or might simply be a matter of preference. In general, if the associated note contains information that you'd like a reader to be able to immediately reference (such as supporting information), use a footnote; if the note contains information that would be more appropriate gathered with other notes in a central location (such as a source reference), use an endnote.

Tip When inserting notes specifically for the purpose of referencing content sources, use citations instead of endnotes or footnotes. You can then generate a bibliography from the citations. For more information, see "Create and manage bibliography citation sources" later in this section.

After you insert a footnote or endnote, you can convert it to the other type of note at any time. You can convert either individual notes or all the notes in a document.

By default, footnote reference markers use the *1, 2, 3* number format, and endnote reference markers use the *i, ii, iii* number format. You can change the reference marker system used by either type of note, set the beginning reference marker, and specify the scope of the numbering change.

You can modify footnote and endnote settings for individual documents

The standard number formats available for both footnotes and endnotes include the following:

- 1, 2, 3, …
- a, b, c, …
- A, B, C, …

- i, ii, iii, …
- I, II, III, …
- *, †, ‡, §, …

You can optionally enter a custom reference marker or select one from the Symbol dialog box.

Numbering options include Continuous, Restart Each Section, and Restart Each Page.

The formatting of reference markers and note text is based on the current document theme. As with other document content, you can also manually format reference markers and note text.

To insert a footnote

1. Place the cursor immediately after the text for which you're creating the footnote. (Do not leave a blank space.)

2. Do either of the following:

   - On the **References** tab, in the **Footnotes** group, click the **Insert Footnote** button.

   - Press **Alt+Ctrl+F**.

3. Word inserts the footnote marker at the current location and in the linked footnote area. Without moving the insertion point, enter the footnote text.

To insert an endnote

1. Place the cursor immediately after the text for which you're creating the endnote. (Do not leave a blank space.)

2. Do either of the following:

   - On the **References** tab, in the **Footnotes** group, click the **Insert Endnote** button.

   - Press **Alt+Ctrl+D**.

3. Word inserts the endnote marker at the current location and in the linked endnote area. Without moving the insertion point, enter the endnote text.

To set the location of all footnotes or endnotes in a document

1. Ensure that no footnote or endnote is currently selected.

Tip If a footnote or endnote is selected, the action applies to only the selected element.

---

2. On the **References** tab, click the **Footnotes** dialog box launcher.

3. In the **Footnote and Endnote** dialog box, do any of the following, and then click **OK**:

   - In the **Location** area, click **Footnotes**, and then in the associated list, click **Bottom of page** or **Below text**.

   - In the **Location** area, click **Endnotes**, and then in the associated list, click **End of section** or **End of document**.

To change the type of a single footnote or endnote

→ Right-click the associated note, and then click **Convert to Endnote** or **Convert to Footnote**.

To change the type of all footnotes or endnotes

1. In the **Footnote and Endnote** dialog box, click the **Convert** button.

2. In the **Convert Notes** dialog box, do one of the following, and then click **OK:**

   - Select **Convert all footnotes to endnotes** to have only endnotes in the document.

   - Select **Convert all endnotes to footnotes** to have only footnotes in the document.

   - Select **Swap footnotes and endnotes** to change both types.

To change the number format of footnotes or endnotes

1. Ensure that no footnote or endnote is currently selected.

2. In the **Location** area of the **Footnote and Endnote** dialog box, click **Footnotes** or **Endnotes** to indicate the element you want to modify.

4

3. In the **Format** area, in the **Number format** list, click the number format you want to use.

4. With **Whole document** shown in the **Apply changes** to box, click **Apply** to change all footnotes or endnotes to the new number format.

To manually format all reference markers or note text

1. Do either of the following:

   • In the document text, select the reference marker for any footnote or endnote.

   • Select the text of any footnote or endnote.

2. On the **Home** tab, in the **Editing** group, click the **Select** button, and then click **Select All Text with Similar Formatting**.

3. Apply the formatting you want.

Create and manage bibliography citation sources

Many types of documents that you create might require a bibliography that lists the sources of the information that appears or is referenced in the document.

Whether your sources are books, articles, reports, recordings, websites, interviews, or any of a dozen other types, you can record details about them and then select a common style, such as APA Style (detailed in the *Publication Manual of the American Psychological Association*) or Chicago Style (detailed in the *Chicago Manual of Style*), to have Word automatically reference the sources in that style's standard format.

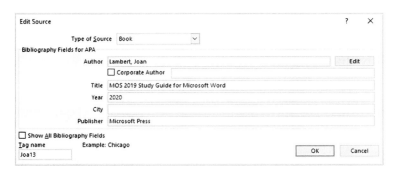

The fields shown in the simple source dialog box are specific to the source type and bibliography style

Tip Currently available styles include APA (Sixth Edition), Chicago (Sixteenth Edition), GB7714 (2005), GOST – Name Sort (2003), GOST – Title Sort (2003), Harvard – Anglia (2008), IEEE (2006), ISO 690 – First Element and Date (1987), ISO 690 – Numerical Reference (1987), MLA (Seventh Edition), SIST02 (2003), and Turabian (Sixth Edition).

If you know the bibliography style that will be used, you can select it to display only the fields required by that standard when creating and editing sources. If you prefer to save all available information, you can expand the individual dialog boxes to display additional fields.

When you create sources, Word stores them in a master list saved in a separate file on your computer's hard disk, so that you can cite them in any document. In the Source Manager dialog box, you can specify the sources that you want to have available to the current document. You can use the Source Manager to help you keep track of sources you use while researching a document, and to ensure that you reference them in the proper format.

Exam Strategy Exam MO-100 requires that you demonstrate the ability to work with bibliography citations. A working knowledge of legal citations is not required for either the Specialist or Expert certification in Word 2019.

4

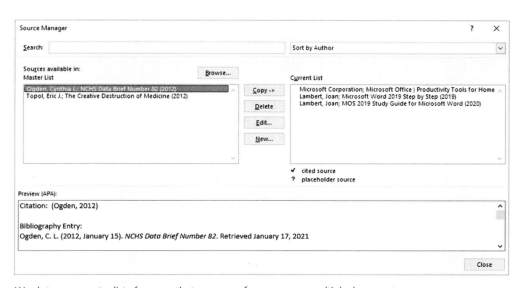

Word stores a master list of sources that you can reference across multiple documents

Citations are embedded references to content and information sources from which you can build a reference table or document. A Word document can include two types of citations:

- Citations referencing content sources, such as books, magazines, and websites, from which you can build a bibliography

- Citations referencing legal information, such as regulations, cases, and statutes, from which you can build a table of authorities

At each location in a document from which you want to reference a bibliographical source, you insert a citation.

There are three ways in which you can create and cite sources:

- Provide details for all the sources, and then cite an existing source.

- Provide details for sources as you insert citations.

- Create source placeholders as you insert citations, and then modify the source information in the Source Manager dialog box.

After you enter citations in a document, you can easily compile their sources into a formatted bibliography.

See Also For information about creating bibliographies, see "Objective 4.2, Create and manage reference tables."

To create a bibliography source

1. On the **References** tab, in the **Citations & Bibliography** group, select the reference style you will be using, if you know it.

Tip The default style is APA. You can retain the default if you don't have another specific preference.

2. In the **Citations & Bibliography** group, do either of the following:

   - Click **Insert Citation**, and then click **Add New Source**.

   - Click **Manage Sources**, and then in the **Source Manager** dialog box, click **New**.

3. In the **Create Source** dialog box displaying the recommended fields for the selected style, select the source type, do one of the following, and then click **OK**:

   - Enter the applicable information in the displayed fields.

   - To save additional information about the source, select the **Show All Bibliography Fields** check box, and then enter the information you want.

Tip In the expanded dialog box, the fields recommended for the currently selected style are indicated by red asterisks.

To create a bibliography source placeholder

1. On the **References** tab, in the **Citations & Bibliography** group, click **Insert Citation**, and then click **Add New Placeholder**.

2. In the **Placeholder Name** dialog box, enter a short name for the source, and then click **OK**.

Tip A source placeholder name cannot include spaces.

To modify a bibliography source placeholder

1. In the **Citations & Bibliography** group, click **Manage Sources**.

2. In the **Source Manager** dialog box, click the placeholder source (indicated by a question mark) in the **Current List** box, and then click **Edit**.

3. In the **Edit Source** dialog box, enter the information that is applicable to the source, and then click **OK** to change the source placeholder to a valid source.

To insert a bibliography citation

1. Position the cursor after the content for which you want to cite the source.

2. In the **Citations & Bibliography** group, click **Insert Citation**, and then click the source or source placeholder.

4

Objective 4.1 practice tasks

The practice file for these tasks is in the **MOSWord2019\Objective4** practice file folder. The folder also contains a result file that you can use to check your work.

➤ Open the **Word_4-1** document. In the *About the Brothers Grimm* section, do the following:

☐ Immediately after the name *Jacob*, insert an endnote that says **Jacob Grimm lived from 1785-1863**.

☐ Immediately after the name *Wilhelm*, insert an endnote that says **Wilhelm Grimm lived from 1786-1859**.

☐ After the name *Hanau*, insert a footnote that says **Hanau is located near Frankfurt, in the German state of Hesse**.

☐ Modify the footnote location so that it appears immediately below the text on page 1.

☐ Convert the two endnotes to footnotes, either individually or at the same time.

☐ Change the footnote numbering format to the range of symbols that includes the asterisk, dagger, double dagger, and section symbols (*, †, ‡, §).

☐ Reposition the footnotes at the bottom of the page.

➤ Return to the beginning of the document and do the following:

❑ Position the cursor at the end of the first paragraph after the heading *About the Brothers Grimm*.

❑ Create a bibliography source placeholder with the name **GrimmData**.

❑ Edit the placeholder source to reference the online article at https://en.wikipedia.org/wiki/Brothers_Grimm. Use the *Web Site* source type. Leave the author blank but complete the remaining required fields, using the current date.

❑ In the Source Manager, verify that the *GrimmData* source appears in the Current List as a cited source, not a placeholder source.

❑ Close the Source Manager and verify that the updated information appears at the end of the paragraph.

➤ Save the **Word_4-1** document. Open the **Word 4-1_results** document. Check your work by comparing the open documents. Then close the open documents.

Objective 4.2: Create and manage reference tables

Create and manage tables of contents

A table of contents (commonly referred to as a *TOC*) after the title or cover page of a document provides a quick overview of the document's content and an easy way for readers to locate specific document sections. A table of contents is particularly useful in a long document. You can include page numbers for people reading a printed document, hyperlinks for people reading an electronic document, or both.

Word builds the table of contents from document content that is styled by using heading styles linked to outline levels. The Navigation pane displays these same headings when you're working in the document.

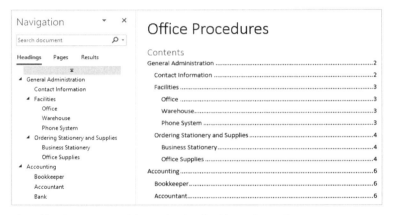

The table of contents provides navigational guidance for readers

Word 2019 has two built-in table of contents styles that automatically generate a TOC based on the first three heading/outline levels. You can modify the settings of either style to include from one to nine heading levels and to use page numbers, hyperlinks, or both. If you include page numbers, you can choose from a variety of page number leaders.

Exam Strategy Exam MO-100 requires that you demonstrate the ability to create a table of contents using one of the built-in styles and standard heading styles. You are not required to demonstrate the customization of a table of contents.

If the content or page layout of your document changes after you insert the table of contents, you must update the table of contents to refresh the headings and page numbers.

To insert a table of contents

1. Make sure that your document contains headings that have Outline Level 1, 2, or 3 assigned to the paragraph styles. If you're using the built-in heading styles, these are the Heading 1, Heading 2, and Heading 3 styles.

2. Position the cursor where you want to insert the table of contents.

Tip If you want the table of contents to be on its own page, insert a blank paragraph to anchor the TOC and then a page break to move the following content to the next page.

---

3. On the **References** tab, in the **Table of Contents** group, click the **Table of Contents** button. In the **Built-In** section of the menu, do either of the following:

    * If you want the table of contents to begin with the heading *Contents*, click **Automatic Table 1**.

    * If you want the table of contents to begin with the heading *Table of Contents*, click **Automatic Table 2**.

Tip The table of contents is contained in one large field. When you point to it, shading appears behind the field content. You can click anywhere in the field to select it. If you click among the entries rather than in the title, a darker gray color indicates the content that will be updated.

To update a table of contents

1. Do any of the following to open the Update Table Of Contents dialog box:

    * On the **References** tab, in the **Table of Contents** group, click the **Update Table** button.

    * Right-click anywhere in the table of contents, and then click **Update Field**.

4

- Click anywhere in the table of contents, and then click the **Update** button located on the right side of the command tab that appears above the table.

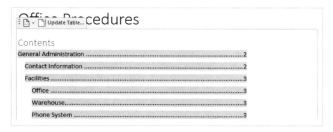

A dark gray color indicates the dynamic content

2. In the **Update Table of Contents** dialog box, do either of the following, and then click **OK**:

- To update the headings and page numbers, click **Update entire table**.

- To update the page numbers, but not the headings, click **Update page numbers only**. You might choose this command if you have manually edited a heading in the table of contents, or if you know that none of the headings have changed.

Updating the entire table ensures that the TOC exactly matches the document

To change the style of a table of contents

1. Do either of the following to display the Table Of Contents menu:

- On the **References** tab, in the **Table of Contents** group, click the **Table of Contents** button.

- Click anywhere in the table of contents, and then click the **Table of Contents** button located on the left side of the command tab that appears above the table.

2. On the **Table of Contents** menu, click the table style you want.

To delete a table of contents

1. On the **References** tab, in the **Table of Contents** group, click the **Table of Contents** button.

2. Click **Remove Table of Contents**.

Create and manage bibliographies

A bibliography lists the sources of content incorporated into research documents, reports, and other fact-based publications that you create. Including a bibliography demonstrates that you've done your research, your sources are valid, and that you're not taking credit for work that isn't your own. If a reader finds that your report contains factual errors, a bibliography can help you to establish that the errors aren't yours.

Most schools and many institutions require that you follow a specific writing style guide (such as APA—the style guide of the American Psychological Association—which is commonly used for content related to psychology, education, and the social sciences) in a bibliography. In all instances, you must reference content sources in a consistent manner, but the details you provide for each source vary by style guide.

You can manually create a bibliography by keeping a list of your content sources and the exact content you referenced from each source, but in a lengthy research paper that can become a big job. Microsoft Word simplifies the process by allowing you to cite sources as you create your document, programmatically generate a bibliography, and update the bibliography after you edit the document to ensure that it remains accurate. In this way, the bibliography feature is similar to the table of contents feature. However, Word's bibliography feature offers one additional timesaving bonus—conformance to all the major writing style guides.

See Also For information about creating and citing content sources and additional information about writing style guides, see "Objective 4.1, Create and manage reference elements."

4

After you enter citations in a document, you can easily compile the citation sources into a formatted source list, with or without a preformatted heading of *Bibliography*, *References*, or *Works Cited*.

Bibliography
Lambert, J. (2019). *Microsoft Word 2019 Step by Step* (1st ed.). USA: Microsoft Press.
Lambert, J. (2020). *MOS 2019 Study Guide for Microsoft Word*. Microsoft Press.
Microsoft Corporation. (2016, September 4). Retrieved from Microsoft Office | Productivity Tools for Home & Office: http://office.microsoft.com

Citations can include varying amounts of information

When you compile a bibliography, Word inserts it at the cursor as one field. You can edit the text of a bibliography, but if the source information changes, it is more efficient to edit the source in the Source Manager and then update the bibliography. If you don't want changes to the source to affect a bibliography you've already generated, you can convert the bibliography entries to static text.

Tip A bibliography includes only cited sources. It does not include source placeholders.

To insert a bibliography of cited sources

1. Make sure that your document contains citations.

2. Position the cursor where you want to insert the bibliography.

3. On the **References** tab, in the **Citations & Bibliography** group, expand the **Style** list and select the writing style you want the bibliography content to follow.

4. In the **Citations & Bibliography** group, click **Bibliography** and then do either of the following:

   - Click **Bibliography**, **Works Cited**, or **References** to insert the bibliography content preceded by that heading.

   - Click **Insert Bibliography** to insert the citations without a heading.

Tip The bibliography is a field. When you point to it, shading appears behind the field content. You can click anywhere in the field to select it. If you click among the entries rather than in the title, a darker gray color indicates the content that will be updated.

To change the writing style of a bibliography

1. Position the cursor anywhere in the document. (It is not necessary to select the bibliography.)

2. On the **References** tab, in the **Citations & Bibliography** group, expand the **Style** list and select the writing style you want the bibliography content to follow.

To update a bibliography

→ Right-click anywhere in the bibliography, and then click **Update Field**.

→ If the bibliography has a heading, click anywhere in the bibliography, and then click the **Update Citations and Bibliography** button located on the right end of the tab that appears above the heading.

To convert bibliography entries to text

1. Click anywhere in the bibliography, and then click the **Bibliographies** button on the left end of the tab that appears above the heading.

2. Click **Convert bibliography to static text**.

4

Objective 4.2 practice tasks

The practice files for these tasks are in the **MOSWord2019\Objective4** practice file folder. The folder also contains result files that you can use to check your work.

➤ Open the **Word_4-2a** document, and do the following:

   ❑ In the blank paragraph after the title (*Office Procedures*), insert a table of contents that has the heading *Contents*. Take the necessary steps to ensure that the page numbers in the table of contents are correct after the TOC is inserted.

   ❑ In the table of contents, note the page number of the last heading (*Shipping Quick Reference*). Ctrl+click the heading to move to that location in the document. Verify that the page number of the heading matches the page number in the table of contents.

➤ Save the **Word_4-2a** document. Open the **Word 4-2a_results** document. Check your work by comparing the open documents. Then close the open documents.

➤ Open the **Word_4-2b** document, and perform the following tasks to modify aspects of the document that affect the table of contents:

   ❑ Change the page size of the document to <u>**5" x 8"**</u>. If this page size doesn't appear in your Size list, you can create it as a custom page size.

   ❑ Change the page margins to Narrow.

   ❑ Go to the *Shipping Quick Reference* section at the end of the document and delete the word *Shipping* from the heading.

➤ Go to the table of contents at the beginning of the document, and then do the following:

❑ Update the table of contents to change only the page numbers.

❑ Note the page number of the *Shipping Quick Reference* heading.

❑ In the table of contents, Ctrl+click the *Shipping Quick Reference* entry. Note that the heading doesn't match the entry. Verify that the page number matches that shown in the updated table of contents.

❑ Return to the table of contents and update the entire table. Notice that the Quick Reference entry now matches the heading.

➤ Save the **Word_4-2b** document. Open the **Word 4-2b_results** document. Check your work by comparing the open documents. Then close the open documents.

➤ Open the **Word_4-2c** document, and do the following:

❑ In the blank paragraph on the last page of the document, insert a bibliography that uses the MLA writing style and has the heading *References*.

❑ Edit the *Grimms' Fairy Tales* source and change the date to today's date.

❑ Update the bibliography.

❑ Change the writing style of the bibliography to Chicago and notice the changes in the bibliography content.

❑ Convert the bibliography content to static text.

➤ Save the **Word_4-2c** document. Open the **Word 4-2c_results** document. Check your work by comparing the open documents. Then close the open documents.

Objective group 5

Insert and format graphic elements

The skills tested in this section of the Microsoft Office Specialist exam for Microsoft Word 2019 relate to inserting and formatting visual elements. Specifically, the following objectives are associated with this set of skills:

- **5.1** Insert illustrations and text boxes
- **5.2** Format illustrations and text boxes
- **5.3** Add text to graphic elements
- **5.4** Modify graphic elements

Many documents will benefit from the addition of graphic elements to reinforce concepts, grab the reader's attention, or make the document more visually appealing. You can insert many types of decorative and informative imagery into a document, including images created outside of Word and images you create or capture using tools within Word.

This chapter guides you in studying ways of inserting and formatting simple shapes, text boxes, pictures, screen images, three-dimensional models, and complex business diagrams.

To complete the practice tasks in this chapter, you need the practice files contained in the **MOSWord2019\Objective5** practice file folder. For more information, see "Download the practice files" in this book's introduction.

Objective 5.1: Insert illustrations and text boxes

You can enhance the content of a document by inserting prebuilt, external, or custom graphic elements. This exam objective requires you to demonstrate that you can insert shapes, pictures, 3D models, SmartArt graphics, screenshots, screen clippings, and text boxes. This topic provides information about inserting and initially configuring those objects. Objective 5.2 provides information about formatting the objects, Objective 5.3 about adding text to graphic elements, and Objective 5.4 about positioning objects and providing alternative text (alt text) for screen-reading software.

Insert and modify shapes

If you want to add visual interest to a document but you don't need anything as fancy as a picture, you can draw a shape. Shapes can be simple, such as lines, circles, or squares, or more complex, such as stars, hearts, and arrows.

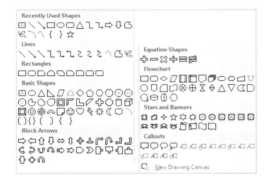

Over 150 shapes are available as starting points for a custom shape

Exam Strategy If the simple shapes that are available don't quite fit your needs, you can draw multiple shapes and group them to create a more complex image. Grouping and ordering objects is not part of the objective domain for Exam MO-100 and you will not be required to demonstrate that you can perform these tasks.

You can enter text inside a shape and apply formatting effects to the shape and the text, together or separately.

See Also For information about inserting text in shapes, see "Objective 5.3: Add text to graphic elements."

You can modify shapes by changing the dimensions, aspect ratio, and—for shapes that have them—angles and line intersections. Most of these changes can be made directly on the shape by dragging various handles; others can be set more precisely from the Format tool tab.

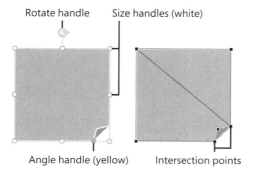

You can significantly modify a shape's structure by changing angles and intersection points

To draw a shape

1. On the **Insert** tab, in the **Illustrations** group, click the **Shapes** button.

2. In the **Shapes** gallery, click the shape you want, and then do either of the following:

   - Click anywhere on the page to insert a shape at the default size.

   - Drag anywhere on the page to draw a shape of the size and aspect ratio that you want.

   Tip To draw a shape with a 1:1 aspect ratio (a shape that has equal height and width), hold down the Shift key while you drag.

To change the angles of a selected shape

→ Drag the yellow angle handles.

To change the vertices of a selected shape

1. On the **Format** tool tab, in the **Insert Shapes** group, click the **Edit Shape** button, and then click **Edit Points**.

2. Do either of the following:

   - To change specific vertices, drag the square black intersection markers that appear on the vertices.

   - To create additional vertices, drag the red lines that define the shape border.

5

To change a selected shape to another shape

→ On the **Format** tool tab, in the **Insert Shapes** group, click the **Edit Shape** button, point to **Change Shape**, and then click the shape you want.

See Also You use the same techniques to manage shapes and pictures. For more information, see "Visually format objects" in "Objective 5.2: Format illustrations and text boxes."

Insert pictures

You can insert a digital photograph or picture created in almost any program into a Word document. Sources for existing images include the following:

- Local images that are saved as files on your computer, on a network drive, or on a device (such as a digital camera) that is connected to your computer.

- Online images that are saved in your OneDrive cloud storage.

- Online images that are available through a web search. Many images can be reused for private or limited commercial purposes under the Creative Commons media licensing. Other images located through a web search might have restricted permissions, so it's important to be careful when reusing an online image in a document.

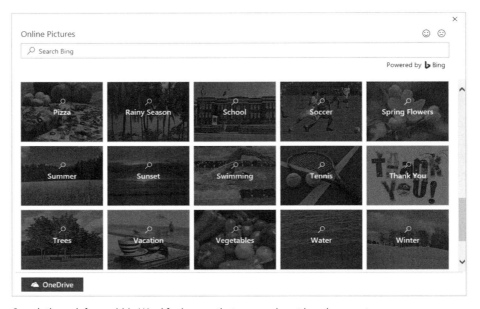

Search the web from within Word for images that you can insert in a document

To insert an image from a file

1. On the **Insert** tab, in the **Illustrations** group, click the **Pictures** button.

2. In the **Insert Picture** dialog box, browse to and click the file you want. Then do any of the following:

   - Click **Insert** to insert the image into the document.

   - In the **Insert** list, click **Link to File** to insert an image that will update automatically if the image file changes.

   - In the **Insert** list, click **Insert and Link** to insert an image that you can manually update if the image file changes.

Or

1. Open File Explorer and browse to the folder that contains the picture.

2. Arrange the File Explorer and Word windows side by side on your screen.

3. In the Word document, click to position the cursor where you want to insert the picture.

4. Drag the picture from File Explorer to the Word document.

To insert an online image

1. On the **Insert** tab, in the **Illustrations** group, click the **Online Pictures** button.

2. In the **Online Pictures** window, do either of the following:

   - To search the web for a picture, enter a keyword in the search box and press **Enter**, or navigate through the categories to the picture you want to insert.

   - To locate a picture on your OneDrive, click the **OneDrive** button in the lower-left corner of the window and then navigate through your folder structure to the picture you want to insert.

3. Double-click the picture to insert it in the document.

5

Insert 3D models

The ability to insert and manipulate 3D models is a new feature available in Word, Excel, PowerPoint, and Outlook. Three-dimensional models are intricate, high-quality images that the document author can rotate in 360 degrees to display the image from any angle.

Three views of the same 3D model of a butterfly

Tip Some 3D models are animated to move on their own. Animated 3D models are most appropriate for use in electronic deliverables in which the animation can be observed in motion. In PowerPoint, you can apply custom animation effects to any 3D model. To keep the discussion in the context of Word, this topic does not include discussion of animation effects.

An extensive library of 3D models is available online depicting a wide range of sub-jects, including animals, scientific processes, emojis, steampunk decor, and origami. You can also create your own 3D models in Microsoft Paint 3D, or work with 3D models that other people supply to you. Word looks for 3D models in the 3D Objects folder of your user profile.

Supported 3D model file types include:

- 3D Manufacturing Format (*.3mf)
- Binary GL Transmission Format (*.glb)
- Filmbox Format (*.fbx)
- Object Format (*.obj)
- Polygon Format (*.ply)
- StereoLithography Format (*.stl)

Exam Strategy The MOS exam environment doesn't allow candidates to access the internet. MOS exam tasks that require you to demonstrate the ability to insert a 3D model will have you do so from the local computer instead of the online library.

To insert a 3D model from the online library

1. On the **Insert** tab, in the **Illustrations** group, click **3D Models** (or click the **3D Models** arrow, and then click **From Online Sources**).

2. In the **Online 3D Models** window, do either of the following:

   - Enter a search term in the search box, and then press **Enter** to display related models.

   - Click a category tile to display models in that category.

3. Locate the model you want to insert, click the tile, and then click **Insert**.

To insert a 3D model from a local folder

1. On the **Insert** tab, in the **Illustrations** group, click the **3D Models** arrow (not the button), and then click **From a File**.

2. In the **Insert 3D Model** dialog box displaying the contents of your 3D Objects folder, browse to the file you want to insert, and then click **Insert**.

See Also For information about rotating, panning, and zooming 3D models, see "Format 3D models" in "Objective 5.2: Format illustrations and text boxes."

Insert SmartArt graphics

When you want to clearly illustrate a concept such as a process, cycle, hierarchy, or relationship, the powerful SmartArt Graphics tool makes it easy to create dynamic, visually appealing diagrams. By using predefined sets of coordinated formatting and effects, you can almost effortlessly construct any of the following types of diagrams:

- **List** These diagrams visually represent lists of related or independent information—for example, a list of items needed to complete a task, including pictures of the items.

- **Process** These diagrams visually describe the ordered set of steps required to complete a task—for example, the steps for getting a project approved.

- **Cycle** These diagrams represent a circular sequence of steps, tasks, or events, or the relationship of a set of steps, tasks, or events to a central, core element—for example, the looping process for continually improving a product based on customer feedback.

5

- **Hierarchy** These diagrams illustrate the structure of an organization or entity—for example, the top-level management structure of a company.

- **Relationship** These diagrams show convergent, divergent, overlapping, merging, or containment elements—for example, how using similar methods to organize your email, calendar, and contacts can improve your productivity.

- **Matrix** These diagrams show the relationship of components to a whole—for example, the product teams in a department.

- **Pyramid** These diagrams illustrate proportional or interconnected relation-ships such as the distribution of time across different phases of a project.

- **Picture** These diagrams rely on pictures instead of text to create one of the other types of diagrams—for example, a process picture diagram with photo-graphs showing the recession of glaciers in Glacier National Park. Picture dia-grams are a subset of the other categories but are also available from their own category so that you can easily locate diagram layouts that support images.

In a Word document, you create a SmartArt graphic by first choosing a layout. The layouts are available from the Choose A SmartArt Graphic dialog box, which organizes them in categories by the type of information they're designed to present. Layouts that include pictures appear in the information category and in the Picture category.

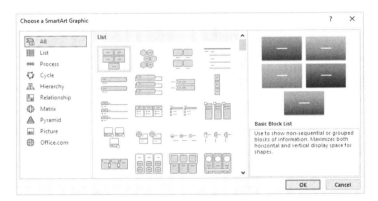

Click an individual category to display only those layouts or click All to scroll through all layout categories

After you choose a layout, Word inserts the basic diagram into the document and dis-plays the associated list format in the Text pane, into which you can enter information. (If the Text pane doesn't open automatically, you can display it by clicking the but-ton on the left edge of the diagram.) You can enter more or less information than is required by the original diagram; most diagrams support a range of entries (although a few are formatted to support only a specific number of entries). You can insert and modify text either directly in the diagram shapes or in the associated Text pane.

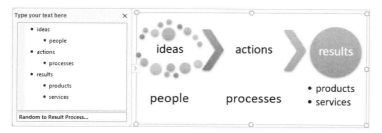

SmartArt text is stored as a bulleted list

SmartArt graphics support a colorful range of formatting options that are linked to the document theme color scheme. When formatting a SmartArt graphic, you can choose to apply multiple colors or gradients of a single color, and you can separately apply two-dimensional and three-dimensional visual styles that range from subtle to very eye-catching.

To create a SmartArt graphic

1. On the **Insert** tab, in the **Illustrations** group, click the **SmartArt** button.

2. In the left pane of the **Choose a SmartArt Graphic** dialog box, click the type of diagram you want.

3. In the center pane, click the layout you want, and then click **OK**.

To resize a SmartArt graphic

→ To maintain the original aspect ratio of the graphic, click the graphic to activate the canvas, and then do either of the following:

- Drag the sizing handles in any corner of the canvas.

- On the **Format** tool tab, in the **Size** group, click the dialog box launcher. In the **Layout** dialog box, select the **Lock aspect ratio** check box, and then change the dimension in the **Height** or **Width** section.

→ On the **Format** tool tab, in the **Size** group, enter or select the **Height** and **Width** dimensions. This method doesn't maintain the aspect ratio.

5

To resize a SmartArt graphic canvas

1. Select the SmartArt graphic.

2. Drag the canvas handles as follows:

   - To increase or decrease the canvas height, drag the top or bottom handle.
   - To increase or decrease the canvas width, drag the left or right handle.
   - To increase or decrease the width and height while maintaining the aspect ratio, hold down Shift and drag a corner handle.
   - To increase or decrease the width and height freely, drag a corner handle.

Insert screenshots and screen clippings

You can capture and insert images of content displayed on your computer screen directly from Word. By using the built-in screenshot utility, you can insert screen captures of entire windows or selected areas of on-screen content.

To capture and insert an image of an app window

1. Open the app window that you want to capture and adjust its height and width to show the content you want.

2. Switch to the Word document and position the cursor where you want to insert the screen image.

3. On the **Insert** tab, in the **Illustrations** group, click the **Screenshot** button.

4. On the **Screenshot** menu, in the **Available Windows** gallery, point to any window to identify it, and then click the window you want to capture.

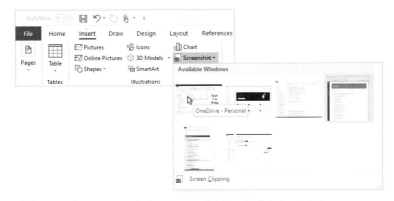

Only currently open app windows are available, not minimized windows

To capture and insert a clipping from your desktop

1. On your desktop, display the app windows and content that you want to capture (you can capture the desktop and multiple apps if you want).

2. Switch to the Word document and position the cursor where you want to insert the screen image.

3. On the **Insert** tab, in the **Illustrations** group, click the **Screenshot** button, and then on the **Screenshot** menu, click **Screen Clipping**.

   The Word window fades and a translucent screen appears.

4. Identify the upper-left corner of the desktop area that you want to capture. Click in that location and drag down and to the right to create a clear window within the screen. When all the content you want to capture is visible in the window, release the mouse button to insert the screen clipping on the document page.

See Also For information about moving, rotating, and resizing images, see "Objective 5.2: Format illustrations and text boxes."

Insert text boxes

Text boxes are containers in which you can insert text that is separate from the text of the document. Text boxes are often used to position sidebars, quotes, or ancillary information on a page. You can draw a text box, enter text in it, and then format it as you would a shape. You can move text boxes independently of other objects, and link them together, on the same page or across multiple pages, so that text automatically flows from one to the next.

Word includes several preformatted text boxes that coordinate with the formatting of other document building blocks (cover pages, headers, footers, and page numbers) and are linked to the document theme color scheme.

5

[Grab your reader's attention with a great quote from the document or use this space to emphasize a key point. To place this text box anywhere on the page, just drag it.]

[Cite your source here.]

Preformatted text boxes may include graphic elements

To insert a predefined text box

1. On the **Insert** tab, in the **Text** group, click the **Text Box** button to display the gallery of built-in text box objects.

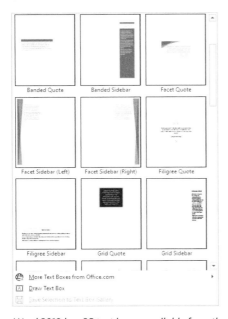

Word 2019 has 35 text boxes available from the gallery and more available online

2. Scroll the gallery to review the options. At the bottom of the menu, click **More Text Boxes from Office.com** to display the additional designs that are currently available.

3. Point to any thumbnail to display the design name and a description of the imagery. Then click the text box design you want to insert.

4. In the text box, select the placeholder text and replace it with your own.

To insert a custom text box

→ On the **Insert** tab, in the **Text** group, click the **Text Box** button, and click **Draw Text Box**. Then do either of the following:

- Click anywhere on the page to insert a dynamic text box that resizes as you enter text.

- Drag anywhere on the page to draw a text box.

5

Objective 5.1 practice tasks

The practice files for these tasks are in the **MOSWord2019\Objective5** practice file folder. The folder also contains a result file that you can use to check your work.

➤ Open the **Word_5-1** document and do the following:

- ❑ Position the cursor in the blank, centered paragraph after the title and first paragraph of text.

- ❑ Insert the **Word_5-1** picture from the practice file folder.

➤ On the second page, do the following:

- ❑ Position the cursor at the beginning of the first blue quote.

- ❑ Insert the **Word_5-1** 3D model from the practice file folder.

➤ Position the cursor at the beginning of the paragraph that begins "Then the king said," and then do the following:

- ❑ Insert an *Ion Quote (Dark)* text box in its default location.

- ❑ Drag the text box to the beginning of the anchor paragraph.

- ❑ From the beginning of the eighth paragraph that follows the third blue quote, copy the sentence "And when the princess opened the door the frog came in, and slept upon her pillow as before, till the morning broke."

- ❑ In the text box, select the quote placeholder and replace it with the copied sentence, merging the formatting. Then delete the *[Cite your source here]* placeholder.

➤ Near the end of the document, position the cursor at the beginning of the paragraph that begins "The young princess," and then do the following:

- ❑ Insert a *Basic Process* SmartArt graphic.

- ❑ Resize the SmartArt canvas to **1"** high and **6.5"** wide.

➤ Position the cursor in the blank paragraph at the end of the document, and then do the following:

❑ Insert a *Scroll: Vertical* shape (from the *Stars and Banners* category) at its default size.

➤ Save the **Word_5-1** document. Open the **Word_5-1_results** document. Compare the two documents to check your work. Then close the open documents.

Objective 5.2: Format illustrations and text boxes

After you insert a graphic element such as a shape, image, or text box in a document, you can change its appearance in many ways. You can move and resize any graphic element, fix its position on the page, and control the way that it interacts with surrounding text. Depending on the object type of the graphic element, you can change its outline or fill color, apply two-dimensional or three-dimensional visual styles, and apply artistic effects. When working with pictures, you can change the brightness and contrast, recolor it, add borders and picture effects, remove background elements, and even crop the image into a shape.

Achieve different results by applying different picture effects

You modify the appearance of graphic objects by using commands on the Format tool tab for that type of object. Selecting a shape or text box displays the Format tool tab for Drawings. Selecting an image displays the Format tool tab for Pictures.

Formatting tools for images   Formatting tools for shapes and text boxes

Similar formatting options are available for most graphic objects

When formatting images, you have more (and more interesting) options. The Picture Styles group offers a wide range of picture styles that you can apply to an image to change its shape and orientation and add borders and picture effects. This group includes the Quick Styles gallery, which contains many preformatted styles that you can apply very quickly. You can select a preset style or select individual border, effects, and layout settings. Effect options include shadow, reflection, glow, soft edge, bevel, and rotation effects.

Choose a preconfigured picture frame or create your own combination of effects

Changes that you make to images in a Word document (such as cropping, removing backgrounds, and applying effects) aren't permanent and can be removed at any time unless you specifically choose to remove cropped content to reduce file size.

Visually format objects

Word provides built-in styles for all types of graphic elements. These styles can include fill colors, borders, shadows, and other effects. If you prefer, you can format individual elements of a shape, text box, picture, or screen image. The colors available in the built-in styles and on the color menus are linked to the document theme color scheme; by using these colors, you can ensure that the visual appearance of graphic elements in the document will stay consistent with other content, even if the theme changes.

5

To apply a built-in style to a selected graphic object

→ On the **Format** tool tab for the object type, do either of the following:

- In the *Object* **Styles** gallery, choose a preformatted style.
- From the *Object* **Fill**, *Object* **Outline**, and *Object* **Effects** menus, apply individual style elements.

To apply a picture frame style to a selected image

→ On the **Format** tool tab, in the **Picture Styles** group, expand the **Quick Styles** gallery, and then click the style you want to apply.

Or

1. On the **Format** tool tab, click the **Picture Styles** dialog box launcher.
2. In the **Format Picture** pane, on the **Fill & Line**, **Effects**, **Layout & Properties**, and **Picture** pages, choose the settings you want to apply. Then click **Close**.

To apply artistic effects to a picture

1. Select the picture. On the **Format** tool tab, in the **Adjust** group, click the **Artistic Effects** button to display the Artistic Effects gallery.
2. Point to each effect to display a live preview of the effect on the selected photo.

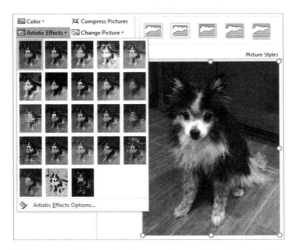

Point to any effect to display a preview on the original picture

3. Click the effect that you want to apply.

To remove background elements from a selected picture

1. On the **Format** tool tab, in the **Adjust** group, click the **Remove Background** button to display the Background Removal tool tab and apply purple shading to the areas of the picture that the tool thinks you want to remove.

The accuracy of the estimate depends on the intricacy of the background

2. Drag the white handles to define the area that you want to keep. The Background Removal tool updates its shading as you do.

3. On the **Background Removal** tool tab, click **Mark Areas to Keep**, and then click any areas of the photo that are shaded, that you'd like to expose and keep.

4. On the **Background Removal** tool tab, click **Mark Areas to Remove**, and then click any areas of the photo that aren't shaded, that you'd like to remove. Depending on the simplicity of the picture, you might need to make a lot of adjustments or only a few.

5. When you finish, click the **Keep Changes** button to display the results. You can return to the Background Removal tool tab at any time to make adjustments.

To discard changes made to a picture

1. On the **Format** tool tab, in the **Adjust** group, click the **Reset Picture** arrow.

2. Do either of the following:

   - Choose **Reset Picture** to discard formatting changes only.

   - Choose **Reset Picture & Size** to discard all formatting and size changes.

5

Format SmartArt graphics

You can make changes such as these by using the commands on the Design tool tab:

- Add shading and three-dimensional effects to all the shapes in a diagram.
- Change the color scheme.
- Add shapes and change their hierarchy.

You can customize individual shapes in the following ways by using the commands on the Format tool tab:

- Change an individual shape—for example, you can change a square into a star.
- Apply a built-in shape style.
- Change the color, outline, or effect of a shape.
- Change the style of the shape's text.

The Live Preview feature displays the effects of these changes before you apply them. If you apply changes and then decide you prefer the original version, you can click the Reset Graphic button in the Reset group on the Design tool tab to return to the unaltered diagram layout.

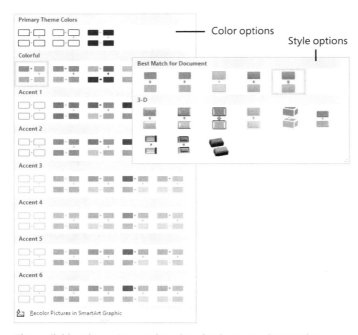

The available color options are based on the document theme colors

To change the colors of the shapes in a selected SmartArt graphic

→ On the **Design** tool tab, in the **SmartArt Styles** group, click the **Change Colors** button, and then click the color scheme you want.

To apply a built-in style to a SmartArt graphic

→ On the **Design** tool tab, in the **SmartArt Styles** gallery, click the style you want to apply.

To apply effects to SmartArt graphic shapes

1. Select the shape or shapes you want to format.

2. On the **Format** tool tab, do either of the following:

   • In the **Shape Styles** gallery, click the style you want to apply.

   • On the **Format** tool tab, click the **Shape Styles** dialog box launcher. Then in the **Format Shape** pane, on the **Fill & Line**, **Effects**, and **Layout & Properties** pages, choose the effects that you want to apply.

To reset a SmartArt graphic to its default formatting

→ Select the diagram, and on the **Design** tool tab, in the **Reset** group, click the **Reset Graphic** button.

Format 3D models

Each 3D model has 18 preset views that you can think of as the perspectives from the outer blocks of a Rubik's cube into the center. The simplest perspectives are Front, Left, Top, Back, Right, and Bottom. The others are combinations of these basic views: Above Front, Below Front, Above Back, Below Back, Above Front Right, Above Front Left, Above Back Right, Above Back Left, Above Left, Above Right, Below Left, and Below Right.

The 3D Model Views gallery displaying the 18 built-in view options

5

If none of the standard views displays the 3D model at the perspective you want, you can rotate it freehand. You can also magnify the model (using the Zoom function) and move it within its canvas (using the Pan function) to display only a portion of it or to put additional space around it.

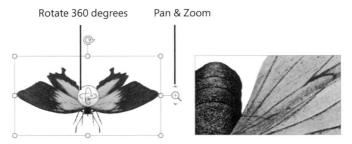

Handles for rotating, panning, and zooming, and the results of doing so

To apply a standard view to a selected 3D model

→ On the **Format** tool tab, in the **3D Model Views** gallery, click one of the available perspectives.

To manually rotate a 3D model

1. Select the model. A rotation handle appears in the center of the drawing object.

2. Drag the rotation handle in the direction you want to rotate the model.

To zoom a selected 3D model within the canvas area

1. On the **Format** tool tab, in the **Size** gallery, click **Pan & Zoom**. A magnifying glass handle appears to the right of the model.

2. Point to the magnifying glass. When the pointer changes to a double-headed vertical arrow (the Pan & Zoom handle), drag up to zoom in on the model or down to zoom out.

   After you release the handle, only the portion of the model within the original drawing space is visible.

To move a 3D model within the canvas area

1. On the **Format** tool tab, in the **Size** gallery, click **Pan & Zoom**. A magnifying glass handle appears to the right of the model.

2. Drag the model within the drawing space to reveal the portion you want to display.

Objective 5.2 practice tasks

The practice file for these tasks is in the **MOSWord2019\Objective5** practice file folder. The folder also contains a result file that you can use to check your work.

➤ Open the **Word_5-2** document.

➤ On the first page, select the picture, and then do the following:

❑ Remove the background from the picture, leaving only the princess.

❑ Apply the *Compound Frame, Black* picture style to the picture.

❑ Resize the picture so that it is **2.5"** wide and maintains the original aspect ratio.

❑ Apply the *Cutout* artistic effect to the picture.

➤ On the second page, select the 3D model of the frog, and then do the following:

❑ Rotate the 3D model to show it from different viewpoints.

❑ Apply the *Above Front Left* view to the model.

❑ Zoom the model within the existing canvas until the frog's nose touches the right edge of the canvas.

❑ Move the zoomed model on the canvas so the frog's head and its front and back left feet are visible.

❑ Use the arrow keys to move the canvas so it doesn't interfere with the blue quote above or below it.

➤ On the last page, select the SmartArt graphic, and then do the following:

❑ Change the colors of the graphic to *Colorful Range - Accent Colors 5 to 6*.

❑ Change the style of the graphic to *Moderate Effect*.

➤ Save the **Word_5-2** document. Open the **Word_5-2_results** document. Compare the two documents to check your work. Then close the open documents.

Objective 5.3: Add text to graphic elements

Many graphic elements support the addition of text. Text boxes, shapes, and SmartArt graphic shapes are all containers into which you can display text.

Insert text in text boxes and shapes

You can insert text within a text box on the page to flow other information around it—for example, to create a sidebar. Alternatively, you can insert a shape on the page and then enter text within the shape without creating a separate text box. You then apply formatting and styles to the shape to control the appearance of the shape and the text within it.

Choose from theme-based formatting combinations or format shape elements individually

To insert text in a text box

→ Click in the text box so that the text box is surrounded by a dashed (not solid) border. Then enter the text.

Tip If the text box contains placeholder text, drag to select it, and then enter the replacement text.

To change the direction of text in a selected text box

→ On the **Format** tool tab, in the **Text** group, click the **Text Direction** button, and then click the direction you want.

See Also For information about moving, rotating, and resizing text boxes, see "Objective 5.2: Format illustrations and text boxes."

To add text to a shape

➔ Click the shape to select it, and then enter the text.

➔ Right-click the shape, click **Add Text** or **Edit Text**, and then enter the text.

◇◇◇

Exam Strategy Linking text boxes is part of the objective domain for Exam MO-101, "Microsoft Word 2019 Expert," and is not necessary to demonstrate for this exam.

◇◇◇

Modify SmartArt graphic content

You can add and remove shapes and edit the text of a SmartArt graphic by making changes in the Text pane or by using the options on the SmartArt Tools tabs.

As you develop the text content of a SmartArt diagram, you might find that the diagram layout you originally selected doesn't precisely meet your needs. You can easily change to a different layout without losing any of the information you entered in the diagram. If a specific layout doesn't support the amount or level of information that is associated with the diagram, the extra text is hidden.

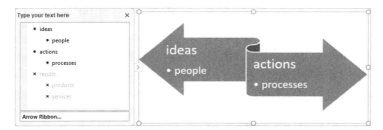

Anything marked in the Text pane with a red X will not appear in the SmartArt graphic

To add text to a SmartArt graphic

1. If the **Text** pane isn't open, activate the diagram, and then do either of the following:

   ● Click the chevron on the left side of the diagram frame to open the Text pane.

   ● On the **Design** tool tab for SmartArt (not the regular document Design tab), in the **Create Graphic** group, click the **Text Pane** button.

5

2. In the **Text** pane, select the first placeholder, and enter the text you want to display in the corresponding shape. The content you enter in the bulleted list appears immediately in the corresponding diagram shape. Then do any of the following:

    - Press the **Down Arrow** key to move to the next placeholder.
    - At the beginning of a list item, press **Tab** to increase the indent level of the current list item.
    - At the end of a list item, press **Enter** to add an item to the bulleted list and add a shape to the diagram.
    - Press **Delete** to remove an unused list item.

3. Repeat step 2 until you've entered all the diagram content.

To add a shape to a SmartArt graphic

1. In the diagram, select the shape that you want to add a shape after.

2. Do either of the following:

    - Open the **Text** pane. At the end of the active list item, press **Enter** to add an item to the bulleted list and a shape to the diagram.
    - On the **Design** tool tab, in the **Create Graphic** group, click the **Add Shape** button.

To remove a shape from a SmartArt graphic

→ Click the shape, and then press the **Delete** key.

→ In the **Text** pane, select the list item linked to the shape, and then press the **Delete** key.

To move a shape in a SmartArt graphic

→ Do either of the following:

    - In the diagram, drag the shape to a different position.
    - In the **Text** pane, drag the list item to a different position.

To change the hierarchy of shapes in a SmartArt graphic

> **IMPORTANT** You can promote and demote shapes only in SmartArt layouts that support multiple levels of content.

1. In the diagram, select a shape.

2. On the **Design** tool tab, in the **Create Graphic** group, do either of the following:

   • Click the **Promote** button to increase the level of the selected shape or list item.

   • Click the **Demote** button to decrease the level of the selected shape or list item.

Or

1. In the **Text** pane, click at the beginning of a list item.

2. Do either of the following:

   • Press **Tab** to demote the list item (and the shape).

   • Press **Shift+Tab** to promote the list item (and shape).

To change a SmartArt graphic to a different layout

1. Select the diagram.

2. On the **Design** tool tab, in the **Layouts** group, click the **More** button to expand the **Layouts** gallery. This view of the gallery displays only the available diagram layouts for the currently selected diagram layout category.

3. In the **Layouts** gallery, do either of the following:

   • Click a thumbnail to change the diagram to the new layout in the same category.

   • At the bottom of the gallery, click **More Layouts** to display the Choose A SmartArt Graphic dialog box. Locate and select the layout you want to apply, and then click **OK**.

5

Exam Strategy Many formatting options are available from the Design and Format tool tabs. Be familiar with the options available on the tool tabs and in the associated dialog boxes.

Objective 5.3 practice tasks

The practice file for these tasks is in the **MOSWord2019\Objective5** practice file folder. The folder also contains a result file that you can use to check your work.

➤ Open the **Word_5-3** document.

➤ Move to the end of the document, and do the following:

   ❑ In the vertical scroll shape, insert the text **The End!**

   ❑ Set the font size of the shape text to 24 points.

   ❑ Align the shape text with the middle of the shape.

➤ Select the SmartArt graphic, and do the following:

   ❑ Between the shapes labeled *Sleeps three nights* and *Prince*, add a shape labeled **Transforms!**.

   ❑ Demote "Eats from her plate" and "Sleeps three nights" to second-level entries.

   ❑ Change the graphic layout from *Continuous Block Process* to **Sub-Step Process**.

➤ Save the **Word_5-3** document. Open the **Word_5-3_results** document. Compare the two documents to check your work. Then close the open documents.

Objective 5.4: Modify graphic elements

Each graphic element that you insert in a document is positioned in relation to a paragraph, margin, or other page element. You can control the position of these objects and the way that text on the page flows around them.

Control the placement of objects within text

Objects on the page can be anchored to a paragraph, be positioned in a specific location on the page, or float independently. The location, position, and text wrapping options determine how the object interacts with text around it. The Arrange group on the Format tool tab for the selected object contains commands for specifying the relationship of the object to the page and to other elements on the page.

By default, Word inserts shapes in front of the surrounding text, and other graphic objects in line with the surrounding text. You can change the position of the object on the page and the way text wraps around it.

The text wrapping options specify the relationship of the object to the text and include the following:

- **In Line with Text** The line spacing increases as necessary to accommodate the object. The bottom of the object aligns with the bottom of the text on the same line.
- **Square** The text wraps to the leftmost and rightmost points of the object.
- **Tight** The text wraps closely to the left and right edges of the object.
- **Through** The text wraps as closely as possible to all edges of the object.
- **Top and Bottom** The text flows above and below the object, but the space to its left and right are left clear.
- **Behind Text** The text flows in front of the object without interruption.
- **In Front of Text** The text flows behind the object without interruption.

5

When you choose a text wrapping option other than In Line With Text, you can specify that an object be positioned in one of two ways:

- **Absolutely** This option positions the object at a distance you set from a margin, page, column, character, paragraph, or line.

- **Relatively** This type of positioning is determined by the relationship of the object to a margin or page.

You can take the guesswork out of setting an object's position by choosing one of nine predefined position options from the Position gallery. These options all implement square text wrapping in a specific location relative to the margins of the page.

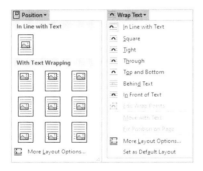

Standard options for positioning objects in relation to the page and wrapping text around them

Even if you use one of the predefined options to position an object, you can move the object manually by dragging it to another position on the page. Often it is easier to drag objects into position if you display an on-screen grid to align against. You can also use alignment commands to align objects with the margins and with each other.

Changing the document text after you position an object might upset the arrangement of content on the page. On the Position and Text Wrapping tabs of the Layout dialog box, you can specify whether an object should move with its related text or remain anchored in its position.

You can also specify whether the object should be allowed to overlap other objects.

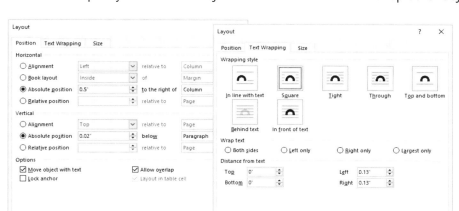

You can precisely control object placement from the Layout dialog box

---

See Also For information about object handles, see "Objective 5.1: Insert illustrations and text boxes."

To move an object

→ Click the object to select it, and then do any of the following:

- Press the arrow keys on the keyboard to move the shape in small increments.

- Drag the object to the new location.

- Cut the object from its original location and paste it in the new location.

To rotate an object

→ Click the object to select it, and then do either of the following:

- Drag the rotation handle (labeled with a circling arrow) to the left, to the right, or in a circular motion.

- On the **Format** tool tab for the object, in the **Size** group, click the dialog box launcher. On the **Size** tab of the **Layout** dialog box, in the **Rotate** section, enter or select a specific angle of rotation.

To resize an object

→ Click the object to select it, and then do any of the following:

- Drag the top or bottom sizing handle to change the height.

- Drag the left or right sizing handle to change the width.

- Drag a corner sizing handle to change the width and height and maintain the aspect ratio.

- On the **Format** tool tab for the object, in the **Size** group, enter or select the **Height** and **Width** dimensions.

- On the **Format** tool tab for the object, in the **Size** group, click the dialog box launcher. In the dialog box that opens (specific to the object type), select the **Lock aspect ratio** check box if you want to maintain the aspect ratio, and then enter or select the height or width.

To position a selected object on the page

1. On the **Format** tool tab, in the **Arrange** group, click the **Position** button to display the standard options.

2. Point to each thumbnail in turn to preview where that option will place the object.

3. Click a thumbnail to move the object to that location on the page.

To open the Layout dialog box

→ Click the **Layout Options** button that appears above the upper-right corner of a selected object, and then click **See more**.

→ On the **Format** tool tab, in the **Arrange** group, click **Position**, and then click **More Layout Options**.

To position an object absolutely

1. Set the position of the object to an option other than In Line With Text.

IMPORTANT The Absolute Position options aren't available when an object is positioned in line with text.

---

2. In the **Layout** dialog box, on the **Position** tab, do either of the following and then click **OK**.

   • In the **Horizontal** and **Vertical** sections, click **Absolute position**.

   • Select the page element on which you want to fix the position of the object (Margin, Page, Column, Character, Paragraph, Line, or specific margin), and enter the specific distance from the element.

To position an object relatively

1. Set the position of the object to an option other than In Line With Text.

   ===

   IMPORTANT The Relative Position options aren't available when an object is positioned in line with text.

   ===

2. In the **Layout** dialog box, on the **Position** tab, do either of the following and then click **OK**.

   • In the **Horizontal** and **Vertical** sections, click **Relative position**.

   • Select the page element on which you want to fix the position of the object (Margin, Page, or specific margin), and enter the percentage difference from the element.

To control the flow of text around a selected object

➔ Click the **Layout Options** button that appears above the upper-right corner of a selected object, and then click the text-wrapping option you want.

Or

1. On the **Format** tool tab, in the **Arrange** group, click the **Wrap Text** button to display the Wrap Text menu.

2. Do either of the following:

   • Point to each option in turn to preview its effects, and then click an option.

   • Click **More Layout Options** to display the Text Wrapping page of the **Layout** dialog box, click the option you want, and then click **OK**.

Provide alternative text for accessibility

Alternative text is descriptive text assigned to a picture, shape, text box, table, or other object that either might not show up correctly on the page or might not be available to screen-reading software. The alternative text provides readers with information

5

about the object content or purpose. In a PDF file, for example, if your content includes alternative text, a reader can point to an image on the screen to display a description of the image.

Readers with low vision or blindness who use screen readers will hear the alternative text for each image the screen reader encounters. If an image on the screen is decorative rather than informative, you can mark it as such and the screen reader will ignore it.

You assign alternative text to an image in the Alt Text pane. You can open it for each image or leave it open while working in a document. The pane content is active only when an image or other object that supports alt text is selected.

Ensure that the alt text describes the elements of the image you want a reader to be aware of

To open the Alt Text pane

→ Select the image, and then on the **Format** tool tab, select **Alt Text**.

→ Right-click the object, and then click **Edit Alt Text**.

To add alternative text to an image

1. Open the **Alt Text** pane.

2. Enter a description that provides the information you intend for a reader to get from looking at the image.

To mark an image as decorative

1. Open the **Alt Text** pane.

2. Select the **Mark as decorative** check box.

Objective 5.4 practice tasks

The practice file for these tasks is in the **MOSWord2019\Objective5** practice file folder. The folder also contains a result file that you can use to check your work.

➤ Open the **Word_5-4** document.

➤ On the first page, select the photo, and then do the following:

❑ Position the picture in the center of the page (using the *Middle Center* position) and then set the text wrapping to *Tight*.

❑ Open the Alt Text pane and enter **<u>Photo of a girl in a fancy blue dress</u>** as the description.

➤ On the second page, select the shape, and then do the following:

❑ Rotate the shape to a position of 330°.

❑ Mark the shape as decorative.

➤ Select the 3D frog model, and then do the following:

❑ Set the text wrapping of the 3D model to *Tight*.

❑ Enter the alt text description **<u>Frog</u>**.

➤ Save the **Word_5-4** document. Open the **Word_5-4_results** document. Compare the two documents to check your work. Then close the open documents.

Objective group 6

Manage document collaboration

The skills tested in this section of the Microsoft Office Specialist exam for Microsoft Word 2019 relate to document markup for the purpose of collaboration. Specifically, the following objectives are associated with this set of skills:

6.1   Add and manage comments

6.2   Manage change tracking

When collaborating on the development of a document, it is useful to be able to identify content and changes contributed by each person. You can do this by tracking the changes that each person makes in the document. Document collaborators can communicate with one another by leaving comments within the document. Comments and tracked changes are collectively referred to as *markup*.

This chapter guides you in studying ways of adding comments to a document, reviewing comments, marking comments as resolved, deleting comments, tracking changes, reviewing tracked changes, and accepting or rejecting tracked changes.

> To complete the practice tasks in this chapter, you need the practice files contained in the **MOSWord2019\Objective6** practice file folder. For more information, see "Download the practice files" in this book's introduction.

6

Objective 6.1: Add and manage comments

A comment is a note that is attached to an anchor within the document content. The anchor can be text or any type of object, or simply a location; wherever it is, Word displays the comment in the right margin of the document.

Word automatically adds your name and a time stamp to the comment

Each comment is inside a container that is fully visible when the comment is active (when you point to or click it). Comment containers are referred to as *balloons*. Balloons can be used for the display of various types of markup.

You can insert comments for many reasons, such as to ask questions, make suggestions, provide reference information, or explain edits. You insert and work with comments by using the commands in the Comments group on the Review tab and on the Comments menu above the ribbon.

The commands in the Comments group make it easy to navigate through and remove comments

Multiple people can insert comments in a document. Word assigns a color to each person's comments and uses that color for the markup associated with comments, insertions, deletions, and formatting changes. (The color is assigned by user name, so if two people have the same user name their markup will be the same color.)

You can select specific colors and effects for comments and various types of markup. For information about this and other features not required by exam MO-100, see ***Microsoft Word 2019 Step by Step***, by Joan Lambert (Microsoft Press, 2019).

Tip Display documents in Print Layout view so that all the collaboration commands are available.

All the comments that are in a document are available for review, regardless of who created them. You can scroll through a document and review the comments as you come to them, or you can jump from comment to comment by clicking buttons on the ribbon.

Tip If a document contains both comments and tracked changes, clicking the Next or Previous button in the Changes group on the Review tab moves sequentially among these elements, whereas clicking Next or Previous in the Comments group moves only among comments.

When reviewing comments, you can take the following actions:

- Respond to individual comments to provide further information or request clarification.

- Mark individual comments as Resolved to indicate that you've processed them, and retain them for later reference.

- Delete individual comments that you no longer require.

- Filter the comments by author and then delete all visible comments at the same time.

- Delete all comments in the document at the same time.

The purpose of each of these options is fairly clear. The ability to mark comments as Resolved is a useful feature. Marking a comment as Resolved leaves the comment intact but minimizes and recolors the comment elements so that it doesn't distract from the document content in the way that an active comment would.

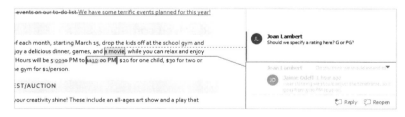

An example of a tracked comment before and after being marked as Resolved

To insert a comment

1. Select the text or object you want to anchor the comment to.

2. On the **Review** tab, in the **Comments** group, click **New Comment**.

3. In the comment balloon that appears in the right margin or in the **Revisions** pane, enter or paste your comment.

Tip Comments are usually simple text but can include other elements and formatting such as images and active hyperlinks.

To move among comments

→ On the **Review** tab, in the **Comments** group, click **Next** or **Previous** to jump from balloon to balloon.

→ In the **Revisions** pane, select any comment to move to that comment in the document.

→ Scroll through the document to visually locate comment balloons.

To activate a comment for editing

→ Click the comment balloon.

To respond to a comment

1. Do either of the following:

   • At the bottom of the comment balloon, click **Reply** to insert an indented response marked with your name.

   • Right-click the comment, and then select **Reply To Comment**.

2. Enter your additional comments, and then click away from the comment balloon to finish.

To mark a comment as Resolved or to reactivate a Resolved comment

→ Right-click the comment highlight (in the text) or balloon (in the margin), and then click **Resolve Comment**.

To delete a comment

→ Click the comment balloon, and then click **Delete** in the **Comments** group.

→ Right-click the comment balloon, and then click **Delete Comment**.

→ Right-click the comment highlight (in the text), and then click **Delete Comment**.

Objective 6.1 practice tasks

The practice file for these tasks is in the **MOSWord2019\Objective6** practice file folder. The folder also contains a result file that you can use to check your work.

➤ Open the **Word_6-1** document and display it in Print Layout view.

➤ Click the **Next Comment** button to move to the first comment shown in the document, which is attached to the word *competitors*. Delete the comment.

➤ Move to the second comment, which is attached to the word *Adequate* in the **Service** column of the table. Point to the word in the table to display a ScreenTip that contains the name of the person who inserted the comment and the date and time the comment was inserted. Notice that the ScreenTip displays more information than the comment bubble.

➤ Click the **Reply** button in the second comment bubble. In the reply box, enter **Please provide details.**

➤ Move to the next comment, which is attached to the phrase *some good*. Resolve the comment.

➤ Save the **Word_6-1** document. Open the **Word_6-1_results** document and compare the two documents to check your work. Then close the open documents.

Objective 6.2: Manage change tracking

When two or more people collaborate on a document, one person usually creates and "owns" the document and the others review it, adding or revising content to make it more accurate, logical, or readable. When reviewing a document in Word, you can track your changes so that they are available for review and retain the original text for comparison or reversion. You manage change tracking from the Tracking group on the Review tab.

— Tracking dialog box launcher

A shaded button indicates that change tracking is active

Tip Turning on change tracking tracks changes in only the active document, not in any other open documents.

Word tracks insertions, deletions, movement, and formatting of content. When you display a document in All Markup view, tracked changes are indicated by different font colors and formatting. The default formatting is as follows:

- Insertions are in the reviewer-specific color and underlined.

- Deletions are in the reviewer-specific color and crossed out.

- Formatting changes are indicated in balloons in the markup area.

- Moves are green and double-underlined.

- All changes are indicated in the left margin by a vertical line.

Moved text is green, and a double underline indicates its new location

As with comments, multiple people can track changes in a document. Word assigns a color to each person's changes and uses that color to format inserted and deleted text. If you prefer to select a color for your own changes, you can do so. You can also modify the formatting that indicates each type of change—for example, you could have Word indicate inserted text by formatting it as bold, italic, or with a double underline, but that change would be valid only for your profile on the computer you make the change on and would not affect the change formatting on other computers.

If you want to ensure that other reviewers track their changes to a document, you can turn on and lock the change-tracking feature and (optionally) require that reviewers enter a password to turn off change tracking.

To turn change tracking on or off

→ On the **Review** tab, in the **Tracking** group, click the **Track Changes** button (not its arrow).

→ Press **Ctrl+Shift+E**.

To prevent reviewers from turning off change tracking

1. On the **Review** tab, in the **Tracking** group, click the **Track Changes** arrow, and click select **Lock Tracking**.

2. In the **Lock Tracking** dialog box, enter and reenter a password to prevent other people from turning off this feature.

Use a password that you will remember, or make a note of it in a secure location so that you can find it later

3. In the **Lock Tracking** dialog box, click **OK**. The Track Changes button becomes unavailable.

6

To unlock change tracking

1. On the **Review** tab, in the **Tracking** group, click the **Track Changes** arrow, and then click **Lock Tracking**.

2. In the **Unlock Tracking** dialog box, enter the password you assigned when you enabled this feature, and then click **OK**.

Unlocking tracking doesn't turn off change tracking; you must do that separately

Usually you would display and review all the markup at one time, but you can also choose to display only certain types of markup or only markup from specific reviewers.

Word 2019 has four basic Display For Review options that govern the display of tracked changes in a document. The settings are:

- **Simple Markup** This default markup view displays a red vertical line in the left margin adjacent to each tracked change. Markup is hidden.

- **All Markup** This view displays a gray vertical line in the left margin adjacent to each tracked change, and formats inserted, deleted, and moved content as configured in the Advanced Track Changes Options dialog box.

- **No Markup** This view hides comments and displays the current document content as though all changes have been accepted. Changes that you make in this view are tracked (if change tracking is turned on) and visible when markup is shown.

- **Original** This view displays the original document content without any markup.

Depending on your view settings, comments are shown in the following ways:

- In balloons in the right margin
- Hidden and indicated by highlighting in the text

You can click the comment icon or point to the highlight to display the comment text.

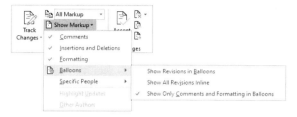

The individual markup display options

After you select a Display For Review option, you can additionally filter the display of markup in these ways:

- You can individually control the display of comments, insertions and deletions, and formatting.

- You can show all markup inline or in balloons, or keep comments in balloons and insertions, deletions, and moves inline.

- You can display or hide markup by reviewer.

To change the display of markup in a document

➜ To switch between Simple Markup view and All Markup view, click the red or gray vertical line in the margin to the left of any tracked change.

Or

1. On the **Review** tab, in the **Tracking** group, click the **Display for Review** arrow.

2. In the **Display for Review** list, click **Simple Markup**, **All Markup**, **No Markup**, or **Original**.

To hide or display all markup of a specific type

➜ On the **Review** tab, in the **Tracking** group, click **Show Markup**, and then click **Comments**, **Insertions and Deletions**, or **Formatting**. (Some devices might have other hardware- or software-specific options.)

Tip A check mark to the left of a markup type indicates that elements of that type are visible in views of the document that display those elements.

6

To display only markup by a specific person

1. On the **Review** tab, in the **Tracking** group, click **Show Markup**.

2. In the **Show Markup** list, click **Specific People**, and then click to clear the check box adjacent to the name of any reviewer whose comments you don't want to display.

Review and process tracked changes

As with comments, you can scroll through a document and review insertions, deletions, content moves, and formatting changes as you come to them, or you can jump from change to change by clicking buttons on the ribbon. You also have the option of accepting or rejecting multiple changes at the same time.

Here are the typical scenarios for reviewing and processing changes that you might consider:

- Display a document in Simple Markup view or No Markup view so that you're viewing the final content. If you are happy with the document content in that view, accept all the changes at the same time.

- Display a document in All Markup view. Scan the individual changes visually. Individually reject any change that doesn't meet your requirements. As you complete the review of a section that meets your requirements, select the content of that section and approve all the changes within your selection.

- Display a document in All Markup view. Move to the first change. Accept or reject the change and move to the next. (You can perform both actions with one click.)

When reviewing tracked changes, you can take the following actions:

- Accept or reject individual changes.
- Select a section of content and accept or reject all changes at the same time.
- Filter the changes and then accept or reject all visible changes at the same time.
- Accept or reject all changes in the document at the same time.

To move among tracked changes and comments

→ On the **Review** tab, in the **Changes** group, click **Next** or **Previous**.

→ In the **Revisions** pane, click any comment to move to that comment in the document.

To display the time and author of a tracked change

→ Point to any revision in the text to display a ScreenTip identifying the name of the reviewer who made a specific change and when the change was made.

To incorporate a selected change into the document and move to the next change

→ On the **Review** tab, in the **Changes** group, click the **Accept** button.

→ On the **Review** tab, in the **Changes** group, click the **Accept** arrow. Then in the **Accept** list, click **Accept and Move to Next**.

To incorporate a selected change into the document and remain in the same location

→ Right-click the change, and then click **Accept Deletion** or **Accept Insertion**.

→ On the **Review** tab, in the **Accept** list, click **Accept This Change**.

To remove the selected change, restore the original text, and move to the next change

→ On the **Review** tab, in the **Changes** group, click **Reject**.

→ On the **Review** tab, in the **Reject** list, click **Reject and Move to Next**.

To remove the selected change, restore the original text, and remain in the same location

→ On the **Review** tab, in the **Reject** list, click **Reject This Change**.

To accept or reject all the changes in a section of text

→ Select the text. Then do either of the following:

- On the **Review** tab, in the **Changes** group, click **Accept** or **Reject**.
- Right-click the selected text, and then click **Accept Change** or **Reject Change**.

6

To accept or reject all the changes in a document

→ On the **Review** tab, in the **Accept** list, click **Accept All Changes**.

→ On the **Review** tab, in the **Reject** list, click **Reject All Changes**.

To accept or reject all the changes of a certain type or from a certain reviewer

→ Configure the review display settings to display only the changes you want to accept or reject. Then do either of the following:

  • On the **Review** tab, in the **Accept** list, click **Accept All Changes Shown**.

  • On the **Review** tab, in the **Reject** list, click **Reject All Changes Shown**.

Objective 6.2 practice tasks

The practice file for these tasks is in the **MOSWord2019\Objective6** practice file folder. The folder also contains a result file that you can use to check your work.

➤ Open the **Word_6-2** document and display it in Print Layout view.

➤ Configure the review settings to display the **Simple Markup** view of changes.

➤ Configure the review settings to display revisions made by all reviewers.

➤ Turn on change tracking. Lock the change tracking feature so that it can't be turned off without entering the password *specialist*.

➤ In the upper-left table cell, select the word *Store* and replace it with **Competitor**.

➤ Display only markup by Joan Lambert.

➤ Configure the review settings to display the **All Markup** view of changes.

➤ Move between the tracked changes in the document and notice that it isn't possible to accept or reject the changes.

➤ Unlock change tracking and turn it off.

➤ Move between the tracked changes and process them as follows:

    ❏ Accept the deletion of the word *much*.

    ❏ Reject the addition of the words *but slow*.

    ❏ Accept both changes associated with the replacement of *Poor* with *Substandard*.

➤ Show markup by all reviewers. Then configure the review settings to display the **No Markup** view of changes.

➤ Save the **Word_6-2** document. Open the **Word_6-2_results** document and compare the two documents to check your work. Then close the open documents.

Index

NUMBERS

A

B

C

Plug into learning at

MicrosoftPressStore.com

The Microsoft Press Store by Pearson offers:

- Free U.S. shipping

- Buy an eBook, get three formats – Includes PDF, EPUB, and MOBI to use with your computer, tablet, and mobile devices

- Print & eBook Best Value Packs

- eBook Deal of the Week – Save up to 50% on featured title

- Newsletter – Be the first to hear about new releases, announcements, special offers, and more

- Register your book – Find companion files, errata, and product updates, plus receive a special coupon* to save on your next purchase

Discounts are applied to the list price of a product. Some products are not eligible to receive additional discounts, so your discount code may not be applied to all items in your cart. Discount codes cannot be applied to products that are already discounted, such as eBook Deal of the Week, eBooks that are part of a book + eBook pack, and products with special discounts applied as part of a promotional offering. Only one coupon can be used per order.

 Pearson